ART NOUVEAU
CROSS STITCH

THE ART IS THE FLOWER PICTURE (see page 94) combines one of Mackintosh's simple, stylised figures holding the familiar rose, with a quotation from a lecture he gave. It continues, 'Let every artist strive to make his flower a beautiful living thing – something...more beautiful, more lasting than life'.

ART NOUVEAU
CROSS STITCH

BARBARA HAMMET

David & Charles

Since this book was first published, some of the fabrics and threads recommended have been discontinued.
Page 54, Tiffany Work-box: Willow Fabrics (details on p 126) hold the remaining stock of the suggested fabric. A good alternative for this project is either Cashel linen 28-count Mint no. 633, or 14-count Zweigart Aida no. 617.
Page 64, The Daffodil Lady: DMC colour 781 has been replaced by 782.
Page 72, Voysey Landscape Clock: Suggested replacement fabric is Fabric Flair 18-count Raindance Blue, no. 18.778.
The Needlecraft Centre at Stable Courtyard, Longleat, Warminster, Wiltshire BA12 7NL, UK (tel: 01985 844802) has a full range in stock and will supply worldwide.

A DAVID & CHARLES BOOK

First published in the UK in 1999
Reprinted 2000, 2001
First published in paperback, 2002
Text and designs Copyright © Barbara Hammet 1999, 2002
Photography and layout Copyright © David & Charles 1999, 2002

A catalogue record for this book is available from the British Library.

ISBN Hardback 0 7153 0837 8
Paperback 07153 1300 2

Photography by Tim Hill
Styling by Zöe Hill
Book design by Diana Knapp

Printed in China by Dai Nippon
for David & Charles
Brunel House   Newton Abbot   Devon

·CONTENTS·

· INTRODUCTION ·

A FOLIO PAGE by Eugène Grasset showing how the characteristics of natural forms could be used to create curving, rhythmic patterns.

THIS BOOK IS A CELEBRATION of the decorative arts of the turn of the last century. There are cross stitch designs inspired by some of the most memorable images of the period and by some of the most influential designers of the time. They include Walter Crane, William de Morgan, Charles Annesley Voysey, Gustav Klimt, Alphonse Mucha, Charles Rennie Mackintosh, Margaret Macdonald Mackintosh, Jessie Newbery, Louis Comfort Tiffany, Eugène Grasset, Seguy and other decorative designers.

Art Nouveau was *the* decorative style at the turn of the century, a style that flowered all over Europe and America in the 1890s, the decadent *fin-de-siècle* years. It made a direct appeal to connoisseur and public alike. It had many different strands and many different names but with hindsight they had striking similarities. Essentially decorative, it was a fresh, ornamental art that looked forward rather than back and it took off like wildfire, permeating all creative fields, including graphics, jewellery, furniture, textiles, even architecture.

As with all fashionable styles, however, its time passed and it had gone out of fashion before World War I. During the 1920s and 1930s a brighter, more angular version of the style known as Art Deco flourished. In the 1960s Art Nouveau style became fashionable again. It was used as the logo of the Biba fashion store and appeared on pop posters and record labels. Today, Art Nouveau and Art Deco influences are being used again in all sorts of household objects.

Art Nouveau never had a manifesto, indeed it took its name from the gallery and shop L'Art Nouveau, which opened in Paris in 1895, showing paintings and decorative objects by modern artists and craftsmen. The opening display included ceramics, glass by Emile Gallé, prints by Aubrey Beardsley, stained glass by Louis Comfort Tiffany, prints by Walter Crane, sculpture by Auguste Rodin and paintings by Pierre Bonnard and Camille Pissarro. There were also prints and *objets d'art* from Japan and the East.

Liberty's was another shop that came to be synonymous with the new style. Described as 'the most delicious emporium in London', it sold Persian carpets, lacquer work, cloisonné, armour, antiques, Chinese porcelain, ivory carvings, lustre dishes, old blue and white Delft ware, clocks, embroideries and lace. They were constantly seeking new products and began to commission designs in the modern style. Liberty's first made its name with its patterned fabrics, notably the peacock feather design, but in 1899 launched its Cymric Art Silver collection, beautiful pieces in a Nouveau style with a Celtic interlace theme. The stunning collection ranged from caskets and flagons to buckles and jewellery. These pieces were mainly designed by Archibald Knox, whose designs inspired two of the small motifs on page 107.

So influential was the Liberty's shop that one of the many names given to the style we now call Art Nouveau was Style Liberty. In Germany it was known as Jugendstil, in Austria as the style of the Vienna Succession, and in Belgium as Style Horta, after the architect and designer Victor Horta. In France it was called Style Metro, referring to Hector Guimard's designs for the Paris Metro. In England and the USA most designers preferred to say they belonged to the Arts and Crafts Movement. There were also a number of more descriptive but less flattering names, like the noodle style or the eel style.

Across the numerous different movements and styles that are called Art Nouveau a unifying feature was a greater awareness of flat pattern and decoration, and a desire to create a new style which took as its starting point not the Academic tradition but a direct response to the natural world. It was an organic style, formed by the imitation of living things; in particular it emulated and formed abstract patterns from the forms of plant life – the sinuous stems, bursting leaves and buds, fertile flowers and sculptural seed heads. Straight lines became curves and curves often

came alive in writhing whiplash exuberance, the rhythm continuing through the whole piece. The tall, graceful ladies who featured so often in these works have their dresses and their tresses swirled and whirled in sympathy with natural forces. Curves, spirals, arabesques and 'S' shapes are characteristic.

A love of rich materials and exciting textures was also characteristic of the style. The rediscovery of Byzantine mosaics inspired Klimt to use gold decoration in his pictures and Tiffany to try to recreate the shifting brilliance of colour and surface in his glass mosaics. Furniture was often inlaid with decorative metalwork plaques sometimes coloured with enamels, as in the work of Mackintosh, Ashbee and Voysey. De Morgan experimented with lustre glazes for his pottery and Tiffany for similar effects in glass. In jewellery, silver was inlaid with turquoise enamels and incorporated mother-of-pearl and opals. Several of the embroideries in this book follow this theme, using metallic threads and filaments to recreate this richness of texture, for example, the designs featuring the white rose and the red rose on page 98 incorporate a metallic gauze.

In order to understand Art Nouveau we need to explore some of the artistic and cultural influences. One of the most important was the art of Japan, which only reached Europe in the mid-nineteenth century after centuries of isolation. It was so different from anything Western, yet so powerful and sophisticated. The style of the Japanese woodcut print with its black outlines and bright, flat colours, its lack of modelling, unusual viewpoints and modern subjects, challenged all the accepted preconceptions. Decorated objects like swords, armour, kimonos, screens, enamelled vases, boxes, and porcelain were all studied and collected avidly. The vogue for grotesque subjects like bats and beetles was borrowed from Japanese art, as well as the more conventional bamboo, willow and waterlily themes. The sinuous ladies and particularly the courtesans provided new subjects in the work of artists like Toulouse-Lautrec. Portraits were painted in Japanese dress, everyone had Japanese fans and decorators created Japanese style interiors. The most celebrated and controversial example was the Peacock Room created by James MacNeil Whistler in 1864, where the walls are painted from floor to ceiling in gold peacocks on dark blue leather. Peacocks, so popular at that time because of their decorative brilliance and Oriental associations, provide the theme for my vivid William de Morgan style rug on page 27.

Japan was not the only new culture to be discovered. The traditional repertoire of Gothic, Renaissance and Classical styles had been enriched by works like *The Grammar of Ornament* by Owen Jones, published in the 1850s. This hugely influential book aimed to make 'all classes, Artists, Manufacturers, and the Public. . . better educated in Art. . .'. To that end Jones published colour plates of the decoration typical of societies from Savage Tribes through Persian and Arabian examples to Celtic ornament. The Victoria & Albert Museum (then the South Kensington Museum of Decorative Art) established collections from all over the world. The Persian influence was an important one on the style and colouring used by William de Morgan. The Bolster Cushion on page 26 is based on his Persian-style tiles.

In fine art, the Impressionists had challenged the certainties of academic art, and a multiplicity of movements and styles had grown up in their wake. Artists like Gauguin wanted to create an art

ALPHONSE MUCHA'S ornamental Art Nouveau style is best represented in his posters for the actress Sarah Bernhardt, where every part of the poster contributes to the decorative effect.

that evoked feelings and ideas instead of just describing the appearance of things. He copied the simplicity of stained glass windows and Japanese prints with their clear outlines and flat areas of colour. He and his group sought to find an equivalent in colour and line for their moods and emotions. The Impressionists had jettisoned outlines: they were reintroduced with more emphasis than before and assumed a vital decorative role in much Post Impressionist art as well as in Art Nouveau design.

The search for more meaningful expression was one manifestation of the Symbolist movement which flourished in the 1990s, led by the poets Baudelaire and Mallarmé but embracing all the forms of art, literature and music. It took its themes not from the visual but from the realm of the imagination – from dreams, sleep, magic, mysticism and music.

The Pre-Raphaelite painters in England with their mythical medieval subjects and decorative emphasis were also an important influence. Edward Burne-Jones had a distinctive style of maiden who was very tall and slender with long, swirling hair and flowing robes. The fact that he worked closely with William Morris and that he designed for stained glass and for tapestry explains his interest in decorative patterning. Dante Gabriel Rossetti's intense portraits of women with their brooding sensuality and symbolic attributes were also an important influence. The femme fatale was to become a common theme in turn of the century art.

The Aesthetic movement, dominated by the personalities of Oscar Wilde and Aubrey Beardsley, encouraged an appetite for decadent and daring art. In its early stages it did much to encourage the pursuit of beauty in all forms, being particularly interested in interior decoration and endorsing the initiatives of Morris & Co

THE PEACOCK SKIRT 1894,
one of Aubrey Beardsley's influential illustrations for
Oscar Wilde's Salomé.

in purveying high quality art objects, fabrics, furnishings, wallpapers, tiles, metalwork and carpets for the improvement of the quality of life.

Aubrey Beardsley was a graphic artist whose black and white images epitomise the *fin de siècle* atmosphere. They are superb arrangements in which the contrast of black and white and of plain unornamented spaces with areas of detailed linear patterning achieve an asymmetric balance learned from Japan. His subject matter is sophisticated, rather naughty and sometimes erotic. Because he designed for the new magazines his work quickly became well known. His influence is seen in the embroidery design for The White Rose and The Red Rose Picture on page 98, where large plain areas contrast with intensively detailed stitched areas.

The fascination with plant and animal life and the stylisation of these into decorative works was a major component of Art Nouveau. Folios of coloured designs were published by various artists including Grasset, Seguy and Mucha. These consisted of decorative treatments of plants with suggestions for their use as borders, stained-glass panels, book covers and wallpapers. Some of these have been used in this book. The sunflower table mats and coasters on pages 20 and 22, for example, were based on a design by Seguy and the columbine picture on page 48 and the snowdrop bed linen on page 78 on designs by Grasset, whose work also inspired many of the border designs on pages 112–118.

Developments in print technology had a vital part to play in the speed with which new ideas spread and became fashionable. Before 1890 all advertising was in black and white, then Chéret and Toulouse-Lautrec began designing colour posters using the lithographic technique and Paris was brightened up with frivolous advertisements for theatres, circuses and cabarets – usually showing pretty girls in a swirl of skirts. Alphonse Mucha began his poster career in 1894 with his first advertisement for the actress Sarah Bernhardt. He became so popular that his posters and decorative panels were quickly printed for sale and made into postcards. One of his champagne posters was the starting point for my design on page 14, a celebratory blackwork image of a woman with luxuriant golden hair.

Printing advances were an important spur to the dissemination of Art Nouveau because they made possible the production of a growing number of magazines on the decorative arts. *The Studio* journal began to publish photographs of works, making a very considerable contribution to the speed with which new ideas, designs and paintings became known all over Europe and the United States. An article in this journal led to the close contacts between Mackintosh and the artists of the Vienna Secession, the Austrian manifestation of Art Nouveau. Klimt was also much influenced by the Glasgow style, particularly the pictures by Margaret Macdonald Mackintosh. The architecture of Charles Rennie Mackintosh similarly became known and important to Austrian designers and architects.

Technological advances in other fields were significant too. The developments in tile making using moulded clay dust made mass production possible, and the technique of printing designs onto the tiles led to the decorative use of tiles in all fields from domestic to public areas like hospitals and railway stations. Many important designers including Walter Crane and Kate Greenaway worked for the tile manufacturers, and changes in fashion were quickly reflected in the tiles offered. The floral designs on page 62 were based on some of Walter Crane's work.

Industrialisation provoked a strong reaction against it, led by William Morris. His well-known teaching that a work could only be beautiful and meaningful if it was the product of the experience and effort of craftsmen, struck a chord with many who were wealthy enough to be able to choose. As well as the goods offered by Morris and Co for home decorations this reaction led to the production of much impressive metalwork, ceramic, glassware and furniture by members of The Century Guild, The Guild of Handicraft and the members of the Arts and Crafts Guild. It also had a decisive influence on William de Morgan whose tiles, dishes and bowls were all hand-painted.

Louis Comfort Tiffany worked in this tradition, employing a large studio of craftsmen. Having chosen glass as his artistic medium he learned all the experts could teach him then conducted his own experiments. When he could not find colours or textures of glass which he needed for his compositions he invented them. As well as his coloured glass pictures he created *favrile* hand-made glass bowls and vases which were manipulated into a variety of organic shapes, often based on lilies and tulips. They were beautifully coloured and textured, often with opaque, opalescent or lustred finishes. A popular patterned finish resembled peacock feathers, created from the blobs of coloured glass that had been added in the molten state. None of the pieces were decorated later: once the glass had cooled the work was complete.

A VIRTUOSO PIECE of glass mosaic. When it was first exhibited, the catalogue explained that the effect was obtained 'without the use of paints or enamels'. Look closely at the goldfish bowl and marvel at the skill! The boughs of blossom are reminiscent of those used in my design for the Bamboo, Blossom and Birds Work-box on page 54.

were made to lean and curve in a rhythmic and unprecedented way. In Belgium, Victor Horta designed buildings on a more domestic scale where he twisted and turned the metalwork into arabesques and curves, used as both support and decoration. Like many of his contemporaries he designed interiors as well as exteriors creating memorable spaces where the decoration of walls and floor echo the curves of the structure to create a totally designed environment.

I hope this brief introduction has conveyed some of *my* enthusiasm for Art Nouveau and gives you a flavour of the decorative art that inspired the designs in this book. It

Tiffany was not by any means the only significant glass artist at the time. Emile Gallé produced many wonderful Art Nouveau pieces using the familiar flower repertoire but also creatures from under the water. Like Tiffany he is well known for his table lamps, a very popular form at the time.

Art Nouveau was a movement that expressed itself on a monumental scale as well. The Spanish architect, Gaudí designed a whole landscape with buildings in the Güell Park Barcelona, where walls

was very popular in its time, a perfect reflection of the frivolity, freedom and spirit of the turn of the century years, an unthreatening art with a direct appeal to the eye and the emotions. It was a time when artists and designers revelled in decorative line, sensuous colour and varied texture. Their subjects were a combination of pretty women, exotic insects and lovely flowers – treated with a dash of stylish abstraction. I hope something of my enthusiasm for this style can be seen in the cross stitch interpretations that follow. ❦ ❦

·POSTER·ART·INSPIRATION·

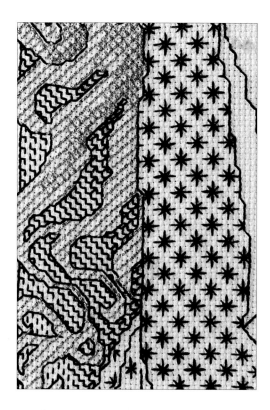

ALPHONSE MUCHA was a poster artist whose works evoke the gaiety and glamour of society at the turn of the century. Hallmarks of his style are beautiful ladies with luxuriant hair, abundant flowers and superb decorative borders.

Born in Czechoslovakia in 1860, he struggled to succeed in the art world, beginning as a painter of stage scenery in Vienna. His breakthrough came in Paris in the 1890s when he was in the studio of a printing firm finishing some work for a friend. The printer had an urgent request for a theatre poster for the actress Sarah Bernhardt, for a play opening on New Year's day. Mucha was asked to help and after a few hectic days designing and drawing onto lithographic stones, the posters were ready. The printer was appalled when he saw them because they were different from anything he had seen before, but the theatre needed them so urgently they were delivered.

Mucha was downcast when he was summoned to see Sarah Bernhardt, but she loved his work and asked him to do all her posters. He went on to design sets, costumes and jewellery for her, notably a gold serpent bracelet set with opals, rubies and diamonds. It was the beginning of a period of fame and fortune. He designed posters for products including cigarettes, beer, champagne, bicycles and train travel.

I have used his poster of 1897 for Champagne Ruinart of Rheims as inspiration for a picture and a card. For the Champagne Lady I have kept the long, narrow proportions of the original poster, but replaced the advertising with a choice of messages suitable for the celebratory subject. The Celebration Card concentrates on the champagne glass and the bubbles. Champagne glasses at the time were wide and shallow, quite unlike the flutes fashionable now.

In the Champagne Lady, Mucha's swirling outlines are stitched in back stitch or double running stitch. The black and gold colouring and decorative nature of blackwork seemed appropriate for this design, so I have translated the areas of colour on the poster into different blackwork patterns.

Blackwork is a traditional counted technique made from the same basic stitches as cross stitchers use all the time. Traditionally it was worked on fine linen but is equally suitable for Aida. All the patterns are created out of basic straight stitches from one hole in the fabric to an adjacent one, either vertically, horizontally or diagonally. ❦ ❦

ALPHONSE MUCHA'S Art Nouveau style is characterised by sensuous ladies with twisting, swirling hair. This Champagne Lady Picture and Celebration Card capture his flamboyant style and flowing lines.

·Champagne·Lady· ·Picture·

Inspired by the poster art of Alphonse Mucha, this lady comes from a poster advertising champagne. Blackwork embroidery is traditionally worked in black silk and decorated with gold or silver thread, gilt spangles and pearls. Here, the black parts are worked with stranded cotton and gold highlights in Kreinik braids. Glass beads represent champagne bubbles and pearly beads add decoration to the stole.

❦

FINISHED SIZE

Design size: 5½ x 15½in (14 x 39.5cm) approximately
(mounted in a 8 x 20 in (20 x 51cm) frame)
Stitch count: 78 x 217

•

MATERIALS

- 14 x 26in (35.5 x 66cm) 14-count cream Aida
(for a larger picture, 7 x 20in (18 x 51cm) on 11-count
Aida use 15 x 30in (38 x 76cm))
- DMC black (310) stranded cotton, 2 skeins
- Kreinik Fine (#8) Braid 002HL, 2 spools
- Kreinik Very Fine (#4) Braid 002, 1 spool
- Mill Hill gold glass beads 02011, 1 packet
- Mill Hill pearl glass beads 00123, 1 packet
- Size 24 tapestry needle
- Beading needle and cream sewing thread

❦

1 Mark the central horizontal and vertical guidelines on the fabric with tacking (see page 120). It is best to work this design using an embroidery frame.

2 Following the chart on page 16, begin by outlining the figure and hair in back stitch or double running stitch (see page 122) using two strands of black stranded cotton. Begin near the centre guidelines and keep checking your position. Continue to outline the panel behind the figure and the glass stem and sides. Avoid carrying threads across areas to be left cream or they may show through: either finish off and start again or thread the cotton through other stitches on the back.

3 Work the top and bottom borders in cross stitch, using two strands of black.

4 Using back stitch and a single strand of stranded cotton, embroider the curving line behind the head, the lip of the champagne glass and the lines of the dress which spill over the step.

5 Following the chart and Fig 1, work the star pattern all over her dress.

Fig 1 To work star pattern stitch, bring the needle and thread out to the right side at 1, go down at 2, up at 1, down at 3 and back up at 1. Go down at 4, up at 1, down at 5, and up at 1. Go down at 6, up at 7, back down at 6 and up at 1. Go down at 8, up at 9, down at 8 again and up at 1. Go down at 10, up at 11, down at 10 and back up at 1. Go down at 12, up at 13 and down again at 12 to complete the star. Take the thread across to the next star.

6 Using Fine Braid work the hair in two stages. Begin with diagonal back stitches which slope from top right to bottom left. Double running stitch is good for these straight lines. Remember that no stitch should cover more than one block of the fabric (on the front). Take care not to pull this thread too tightly. Parts of her hair have a second diagonal back stitch worked from top left to bottom right: work those parts next.

7 The background pattern is built up from straight lines worked in two strands of black, using a blackwork

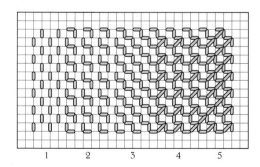

Fig 2 The background stitching pattern, building up with straight stitches from the lightest tone of part 1 to the darkest of part 5.

pattern to achieve a gradual tonal variation. Follow the chart closely for the various parts (see Fig 2 for details). Part 5 of Fig 2 shows the additional diagonal pattern needed to achieve the darkest tone around the head and left side of the body.

8   Work the facial features, using a single strand of black to define the nose and the outside of the lips and two strands elsewhere. Work the shading under her left elbow with one strand.

9   Using Very Fine Braid, work the cross stitch champagne in the glass and then work a greeting from those charted on page 18. If none of these suit you then you could create your own greeting.

10   Remove the guidelines, press carefully then sew on the beads using the beading needle and cream sewing thread (see chart and Fig 3). To finish, mount and frame your picture (see page 123).

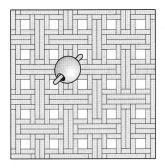

Fig 3 Attaching a bead.

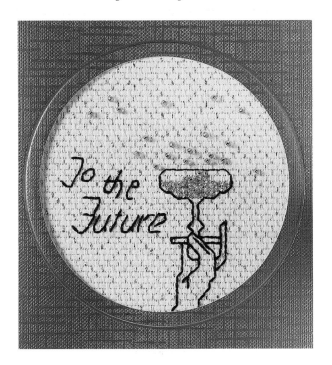

·Celebration·Card·

M ucha was an expert at representing gaiety, glamour and celebration, and nothing is as celebratory as a glass of champagne. Here, the bubbles are represented by little gold glass beads.

FINISHED SIZE
Design size: To fit a 3¼in (8.25cm) diameter
aperture card
Stitch count: 35 x 38

MATERIALS
• 4 x 6in (10 x 15cm) 14-count Aida gold fleck,
code 118
• DMC black (310) stranded cotton, a small amount
• Kreinik Very Fine (#4) Braid 002, a small amount
• Mill Hill gold glass beads 02011, a few
• Size 24 tapestry needle
• Beading needle and cream sewing thread
• Gold three-fold card with 3¼in (8.25cm)
circular aperture
• Double-sided adhesive tape

1   Place the card over the piece of Aida and mark the centre of the aperture with a pin.

2   Following the chart on page 18, begin at the centre and stitch the design using two strands of black stranded cotton for all the back stitch (except the top of the glass which uses one strand) and a single strand of Very Fine Braid for the cross stitch.

3   Sew on the gold beads to complete the embroidery then attach to the card with double-sided adhesive tape.

Variations

❦   The Champagne Lady design could also be used to celebrate a golden wedding anniversary or a special birthday.

❦   You could work the Champagne Lady design in cross stitch rather than blackwork, working the outlines and then filling in with cross stitch. Use a gold colour for the hair and choose other colours for the dress and stole.

CHAMPAGNE LADY PICTURE

Work your greeting here, choosing one of those charted on page 18.

Blackwork in: Beads: Mill Hill Seed Beads

———— Black   310   ⦾ Pearl   00123

———— Fine Braid   002HL(#8)   • Victoria Gold   02011

———— Very Fine Braid 002(#4)

VARIOUS GREETINGS which could be used on the Champagne Lady Picture.

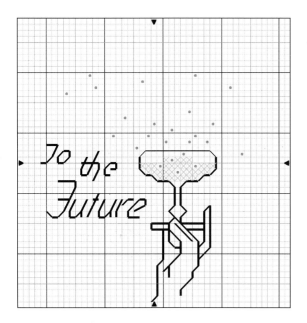

CELEBRATION CARD

Blackwork in:

——— Black   310

——— Very Fine Braid 002(#4)

Beads: Mill Hill Seed Beads

● Victoria Gold   02011

CHAMPAGNE LADY

Blackwork in:

——— Black   310

——— Fine Braid   002HL(#8)

——— Very Fine Braid 002(#4)

Beads: Mill Hill Seed Beads

● Pearl   00123

● Victoria Gold   02011

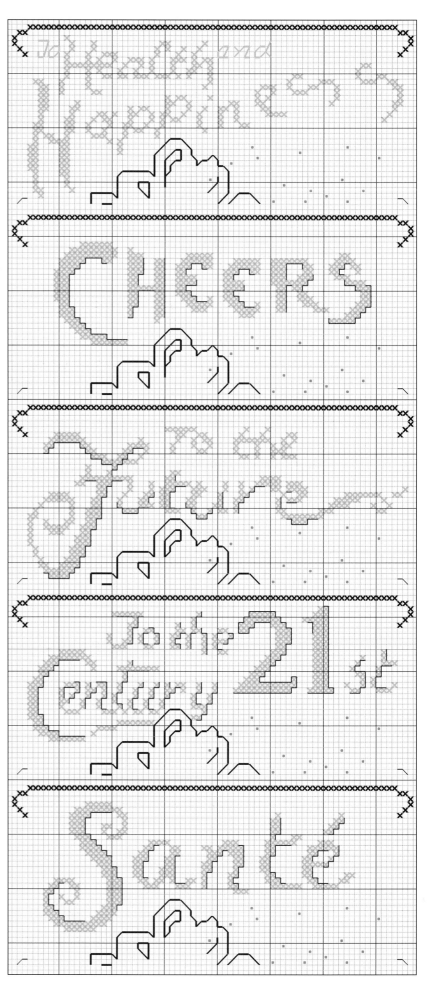

·ASYMMETRICAL·FLORAL·DESIGN·

THE BOLD SUNFLOWERS that inspired this table mats and coasters set were adapted from a decorative border design by French designer E. A. Seguy, from his album *Les Fleurs et Leurs Applications Décoratives*, published in 1901.

Sunflowers have always seemed to be popular but they were particular favourites of artists in the second half of the nineteenth century. William Morris loved them and the potter, William de Morgan, created numerous sunflower tile designs. Images of the plant were commonly used to decorate exteriors as well, and as a motif for stucco decoration and even ironwork. Oscar Wilde made the sunflower the symbol of the Aesthetic Movement, popular in the 1880s and 1890s. In France, Van Gogh painted them repeatedly. Around the turn of the century, the Symbolist artists used the sunflower as a symbol of the sun and thus of the life force. In fact they were renewing a very old tradition as the Incas of South America revered the sunflower as the emblem of their sun god. It was one of the first American plants to be brought back to Europe.

I particularly liked Seguy's sunflowers – their vitality and energy, their curving, curling stems and sun-dried leaves. I also wanted to recreate the asymmetrical look of Art Nouveau work. A love of asymmetry was one of the features Art Nouveau artists learned from the Japanese prints they admired so much. For the table mat design, I isolated a simple group of sunflowers, which in the original Seguy design is repeated over and over. This lent itself to an asymmetrical arrangement that decorates the part of the mat which, when in use, is not obscured by crockery.

·Sunflower·Table·Mat·

These attractive and useful table mats and coasters use a rayon and cotton mix fabric from Zweigart called Meran, which looks like linen. At 27 threads to the inch it is much easier to stitch than linen and has a very attractive texture. It is also available in a lovely range of colours. I chose to make a simple machined hem on the mat but you could create a fringed edge instead.

❦

FINISHED SIZE
17 x 14in (43.3 x 35.5cm) approximately

•

MATERIALS (for one table mat)
• 20 x 17in (50 x 43cm) 27-count Zweigart Meran in light jade, code 695 (The fabric is 55in (140cm) wide, so 1m would be sufficient for six mats and lots of coasters)
• Stranded cottons as listed in the key
• Size 24 tapestry needle

❦

1   With a machine zigzag stitch or hand sewing, neaten the cut edges of the fabric as it frays easily. Mark the finished size of the table mat on the fabric with pins or a row of tacking stitches (see Fig 1).

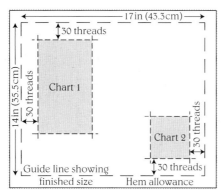

Fig 1 The layout of the table mat motifs.

INSPIRED BY THE WORK of E. A. Seguy, these intensely coloured sunflowers contrast with a lovely light jade fabric to create these table mats and matching coasters. The fabric was selected to contrast with the yellows and oranges, but also because it looks good with a wide range of tableware and most wooden surfaces.

2 Find the starting point for the embroidery by carefully counting in from the marked edges. From the top left-hand corner count down thirty threads, or measure 1¹⁄₁₀in (2.7cm), marking the position with tacking stitches (see Fig 1). Repeat, counting from the left-hand guideline. Mark the bottom right corner in a similar way to establish the edges of the two charts.

3 Stitch the design following the two charts on page 23 and using two strands of stranded cotton over two fabric threads. For one mat you will need most of one skein of yellow and russet and a little of the orange and copper.

4 When the embroidery is complete, press the fabric (see page 121). Fold the edges along the guidelines and press the crease. Remove any tacking and using a sewing thread that matches the fabric, make a neat hem with mitred corners (see page 124).

·Sunflower·Coaster·

This coaster design is very similar to the right-hand flower on the table mat, but as I wanted to echo the burnt orange of the stems I added this colour to the petals for accent.

DESIGN SIZE
Each coaster 3¼in (8.25cm) diameter approximately
Stitch count: 33 x 32

•

MATERIALS (for one coaster)
• 6 x 6in (15 x 15cm) 27-count Zwiegart Meran, colour 695 (or see table mat materials page 20)
• Stranded cottons as listed in the key
• Size 24 tapestry needle
• Scrap of iron-on interfacing
• Round glass coasters with wooden bases
(see Suppliers page 126)

1 Using a machine zigzag stitch or hand sewing, neaten the cut edges of the fabric to prevent fraying and fold to find the centre point.

2 Working from the centre outwards and following the chart below, begin stitching the design using two strands of stranded cotton over two threads of the fabric. You should be able to use threads left over from stitching the table mats.

3 When the embroidery is complete, press and then iron the interfacing to the back so that the fabric can be trimmed without fraying.

4 Position the design in the middle of the coaster then cut out the fabric using the template provided. Assemble the coaster according to the manufacturer's instructions.

SUNFLOWER TABLE MAT AND COASTER KEY

Colour	DMC	Anchor	Madeira
Yellow	972	298	0107
Burnt orange	720	326	0309
Copper	919	340	0313
Dark russet	3777	1015	0407

SUNFLOWER COASTER

DMC

▧ 972

▨ 720

◼ 3777

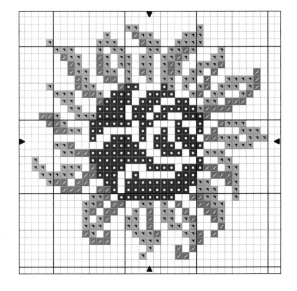

CHART 1

CHART 2

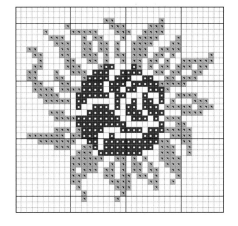

SUNFLOWER TABLE MAT

DMC

◣	972
◪	720
◳	919
◼	3777

·INSPIRED·BY·PERSIA·
·AND·PEACOCKS·

THIS GLORIOUS RUG
AND BOLSTER cushion
were inspired by the
Persian-style tile designs of
William de Morgan. The pea-
cock was used in all the decorative arts at the time
and William de Morgan used them over and over.
I love his decorative patterning and find his lumi-
nous blues and turquoises so attractive that
I wanted to achieve a similar richness in stitches.

Decorative tiles were enormously fashionable in
the late nineteenth century. Tile panels were
sometimes framed like pictures or applied to walls
surrounded by a complex arrangement of plain
and patterned tiles. De Morgan designed these
schemes for public and private buildings and
many of the great ocean liners.

He began designing in ceramics when he
worked for Morris and Co but he soon established
his own workshop and unique style. By the 1880s
de Morgan was producing a range of ceramics
in his Persian style, incorporating the typical
ogee and palmette shapes, stylised flowers and
leaves, all in glowing colours. He had begun by
imitating imported tiles for Lord Leighton's Arab
Hall, but quickly personalised the style, which
remained a favourite in his extensive repertoire
which also included flowers, all sorts of birds and
animals and sailing ships, often with decorative
fish or sea monsters. ❦ ❦

*WILLIAM DE MORGAN'S pottery is a feast for the
senses, with its lovely flowing patterns and rich, luminous
colours. His tile designs were the inspiration for this
Peacock Rug and Bolster Cushion.*

·Bolster·Cushion·

I wanted to make a bolster cushion which would accompany the peacock rug, to suggest the Turkish-style interiors popular at the end of the nineteenth century with their couches, divans and heaps of cushions. This arrangement was inspired by one of William de Morgan's two tile border designs which showed the dark flower on one and the light on the next. Using decorative bands applied to a plain cushion cover fabric makes a small area of intense pattern go a long way!

❧

DESIGN SIZES

Wide border 3½ x 22½in (9 x 57cm);
Narrow border 1¼ x 22½in (3 x 57cm)
Stitch counts: Wide border 314 x 49;
Narrow border 314 x 16

•

MATERIALS

• 12 x 27½in (30 x 70cm) 14-count Permin Aida in rue green (or Zweigart sage green, code 611)
• Stranded cottons as listed in the key
• Tapestry needle size 24
• White iron-on interfacing
• Cushion pad 20in (51cm) long x 8in (20cm) diameter
• Fabric for cushion cover, minimum 24 x 36in (60 x 90cm) in a strong, plain colour to complement the design
• Narrow braid and piping cord to match the design
• 2 tassels (optional)

❧

1 Mark the central horizontal and vertical guidelines on the fabric with tacking (see page 120).

2 Follow the charts on pages 36 and 37 and work the two borders side by side along the length of the fabric, leaving 2in (5cm) between them so that you can cut them apart when embroidered. The design is worked with two strands of stranded cotton and cross stitch throughout. A leaf has been added at either end to fill the gap around the join. If you need to adjust the size slightly to fit your cushion pad then leave out that leaf.

3 When you have stitched both designs, iron the interfacing onto the back and separate the designs,

trimming both strips to a line six blocks out from the widest part of the design.

4 Make the cushion cover by first cutting out the cover fabric to make one rectangle 21 x 24in (54 x 61cm) and two circles 9½in (24cm) diameter. Place the two borders vertically on the 21in (54cm) length of the fabric (see Fig 3). Neaten the border edges by stitching lengths of narrow (1cm) braid on either side of the embroidered pieces (mine matched the light turquoise of the design), leaving a three-block border on either side of the designs.

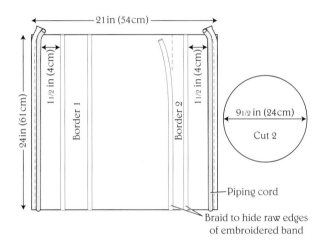

Fig 3 Positioning the piping cord and braid.

5 Check the length of your cushion pad and stitch piping cord to the left and right ends as shown in Fig 3. This is optional but produces a good finish. Arrange the two embroidered borders on the fabric, leaving a gap of about 1½in (4cm) at either end between the piping and the edge of the braid-trimmed Aida. Stitch the borders in place using matching sewing cotton.

6 Fold the fabric in half, right side inside, and pin together at the ends to make a tube, lining up the borders. Stitch a short distance along from either end, leaving a gap large enough to insert the cushion pad. Press the seam open.

7 Pin and stitch the circular end pieces in place, stitching close up to the piping cord. As a finishing touch add two tassels (or make them from some of the remaining threads) sewing one in the centre of each end. Insert the cushion pad and neatly stitch the gap closed.

·Peacock·Rug·

The peacock for this rug was the left part of a decorative tile panel designed by William de Morgan showing the peacock repeated as a mirror image to the right with a vase of flowers filling the space between the two bird's tails. I adapted the design by omitting the vase of flowers and filling the space with more vine leaves. The border design repeats the leaf-strewn paving in the original. A striped outer border picks up the colours of the peacock. The rug is large, but grows quite quickly on 7-count canvas.

DESIGN SIZE
53 x 29in (134 x 73cm) approximately
Stitch count: 389 x 213

•

MATERIALS
• 60 x 36in (150 x 90cm) 7-count Zweigart interlock
canvas (code 699)
• Tapestry wools as listed in the key
• Tapestry needle size 18

1   Centre the design on the canvas by marking the horizontal and vertical centre lines and finished size on the canvas with a marker pen. Mark the line of the edge of the border. The rug in the illustration was worked without a frame (and did not distort at all) and it is more manage-able if it can be rolled as you work. Be careful not to pull the wool so tight that it distorts the mesh of the canvas.

2   Following the charts on pages 28–35 and Fig 1 below, use one strand of tapestry wool and cross stitch over one thread of the canvas. Work with lengths of wool about 20in (50cm) to avoid tangling. By using several needles you can have various colours ready to work in multicoloured areas. It may be easier to work some of the outlines before filling in the details.

| Chart 1 | Chart 2 | Chart 3 | Chart 4 |
| Chart 5 | Chart 6 | Chart 7 | Chart 8 |

Fig 1 Layout of rug charts.

3   Leave the outer borders until last. I suggest turning in the edges and stitching over the double thickness, but you may prefer to stitch to the edge then stretch (see page 121) and back your rug or neaten with a tape.

4   To finish your rug without a visible hem, trim to six threads beyond the marked edge all round, then fold the extra canvas under along the rug edge, making sure the threads line up exactly. A few stitches in sewing thread at the corners to hold in position may be helpful (the woollen cross stitches will cover them). First mitre the corners (see Fig 2) but before cutting away the excess canvas at the corners, reinforce the threads which meet at the corner by stitching over them for a short distance using a close zigzag stitch on your sewing machine.

5   Work cross stitch in colours according to the chart over the double thickness of canvas. The outermost row should be left until last and worked in plaited cross stitch edging (see page 123) which gives a neat finish. It is possible to do this at the beginning of the stitching of the rug but leaving it until the end means that any counting errors can be accomodated.

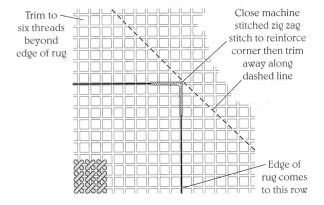

Trim to six threads beyond edge of rug

Close machine stitched zig zag stitch to reinforce corner then trim away along dashed line

Edge of rug comes to this row

Fig 2 Reinforcing the rug corner before mitring.

Variations

❦   The peacock rug could be displayed over the back of a couch or used as a wall hanging. The decorative bars intended for hanging quilts could be used if some tape loops were sewn to the top edge of the embroidery.

❦   You could use the bolster borders to decorate a square or circular cushion or use one alone on an Aida or linen band for a belt, bookmark, hat band or camera strap.

❦   The borders could also be used in combination with others from the border section on pages 112–118.

CHART 1

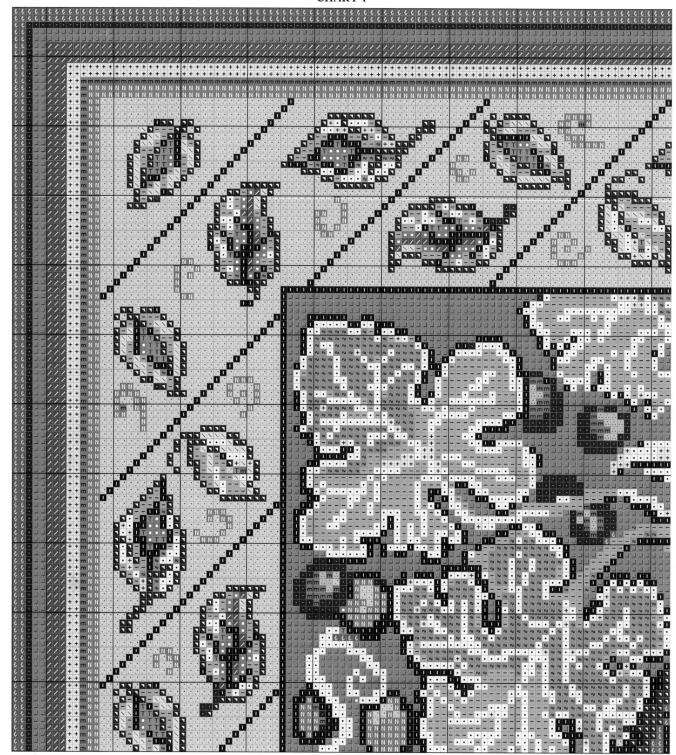

PEACOCK RUG

Anchor Tappiserie Wool

·	8006	⌐	8688	╲	8812	N	8920
∴	8586	ℓ	8690	╲	8820	—	9014
▥	8590	◣	8694	╱	8822	~	9016
▦	8596	T	8806	∴	8874	+	9772
Ɛ	8672	☐	8808	▐	8884		

CHART 2

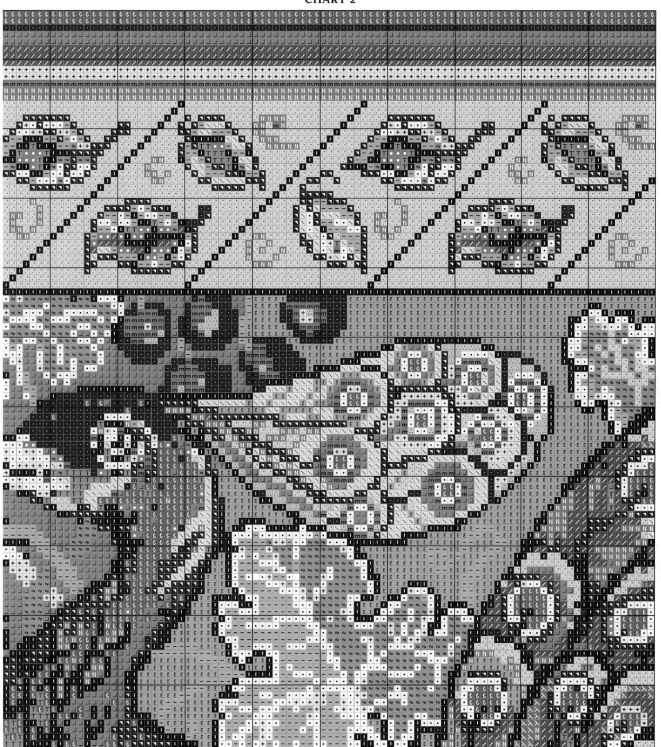

PEACOCK RUG KEY

Colour	Anchor Tappiserie wool	Skeins	Colour	Anchor Tappiserie wool	Skeins
Cream	8006 *	20	Very pale sky blue	8812 *	8
Light lilac	8586	1	Dark sky blue	8820	4
Lilac	8590	6	Very dark sky blue	8822 *	20
Very dark lilac	8596	9	Very light gobelin green	8874 *	48
Light sea blue	8672	9	Very dark gobelin green	8884 *	28
Light cornflower blue	8688	20	Peacock green	8920	13
Cornflower blue	8690	15	Very light forest green	9014	11
Very dark cornflower blue	8694	16	Light forest green	9016	9
Turquoise	8806	3	Light granite	9772	9
Dark turquoise	8808	8			

* These colours can be ordered in 20g hanks, in which case
divide the number of skeins by 4.

CHART 3

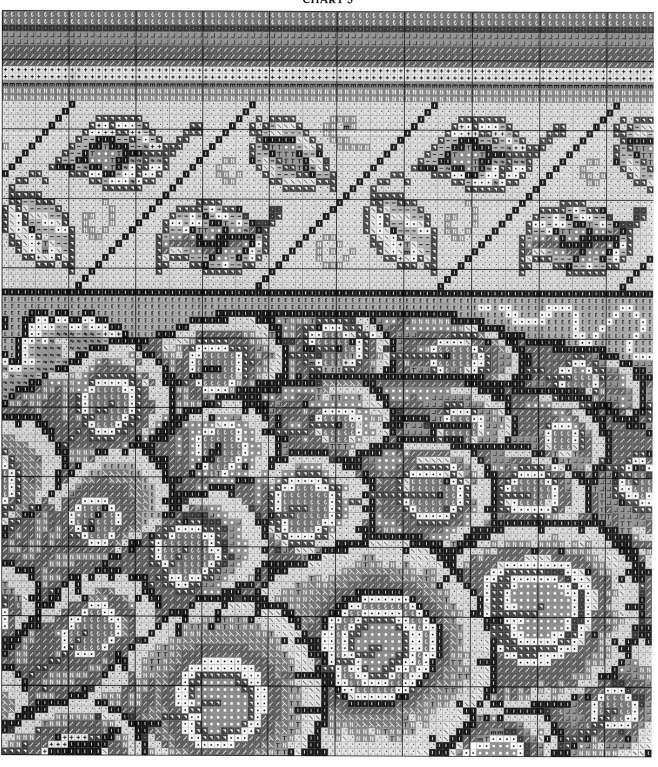

Anchor Tappiserie Wool

· 8006	■ 8596	ℓ 8690	□ 8808	⊿ 8822	N 8920	+ 9772
∴ 8586	ε 8672	◤ 8694	＼ 8812	· 8874	− 9014	
m 8590	◢ 8688	T 8806	⊠ 8820	▮ 8884	~ 9016	

CHART 4

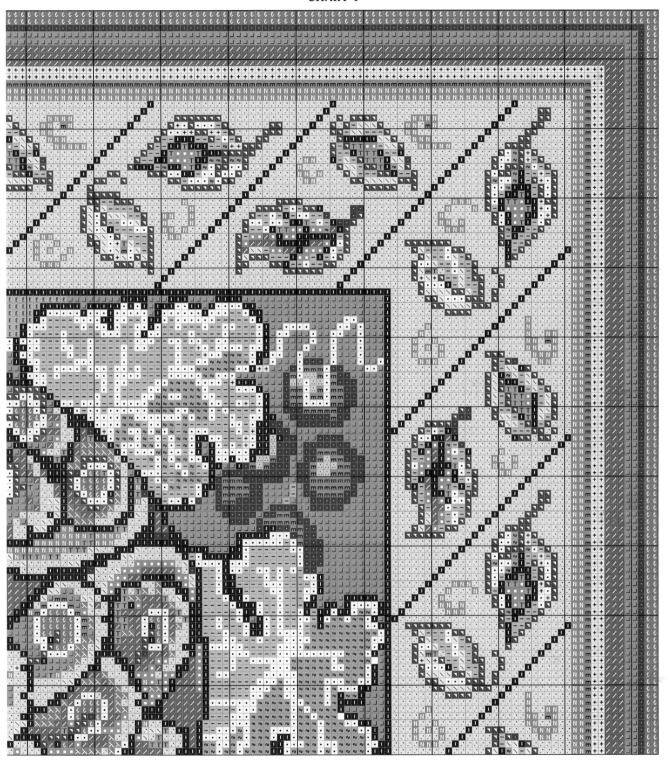

CHART 5

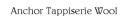
Anchor Tappiserie Wool

· 8006	▪ 8596	ℓ 8690	▢ 8808	↗ 8822	N 8920	+ 9772
⋰ 8586	Ɛ 8672	◣ 8694	◺ 8812	⁖ 8874	− 9014	
▥ 8590	▦ 8688	T 8806	⤫ 8820	▮ 8884	~ 9016	

CHART 6

CHART 7

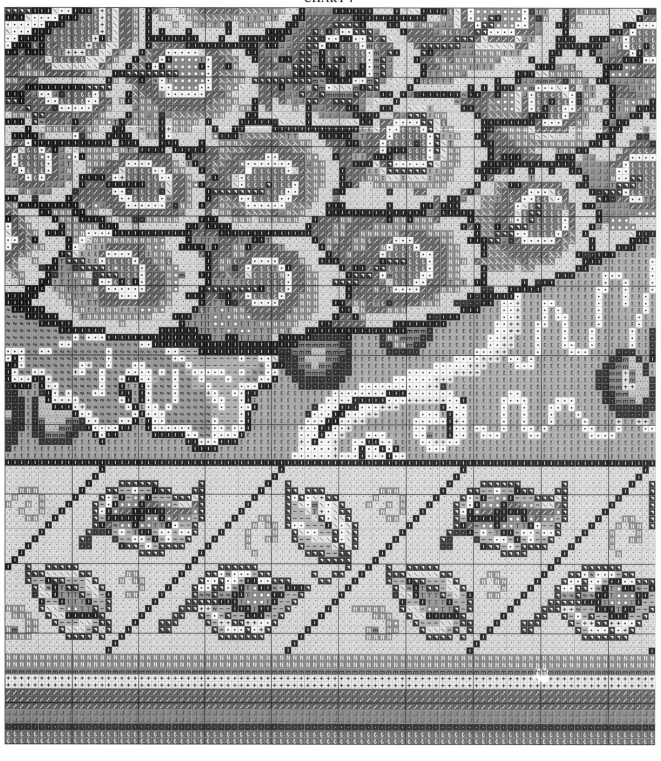

Anchor Tappiserie Wool

·	8006	·	8596	ℓ	8690	□	8808	↗	8822	N	8920	+	9772
·	8586	Ɛ	8672	◣	8694	＼	8812	·	8874	−	9014		
m	8590	⌐	8688	T	8806	⋉	8820	I	8884	∾	9016		

CHART 8

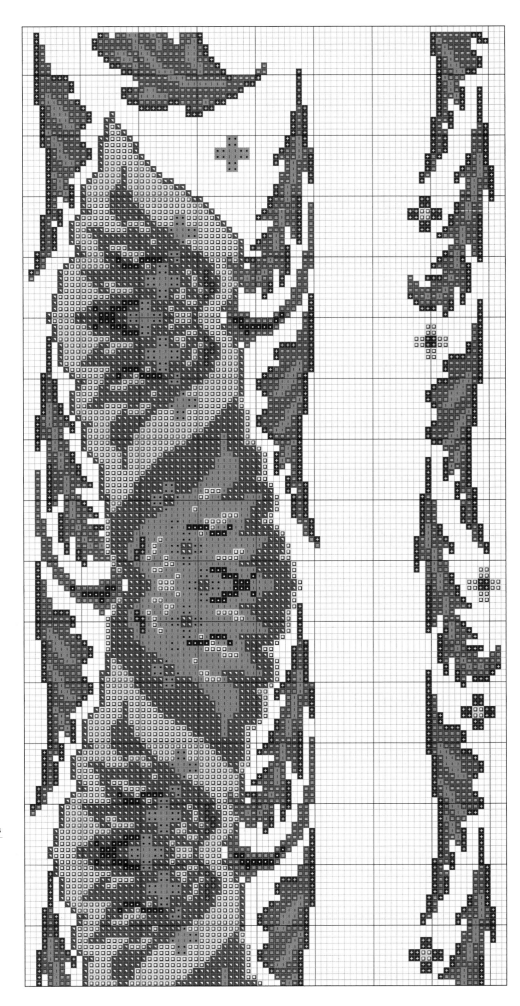

BOLSTER CUSHION KEY

Colour	DMC	Anchor	Skeins
Blue	798	132	3
Green	3814	189	2
Pale blue	3756	1037	2
Light turquoise	3766	167	2
Dark turquoise	3765	169	2
Lilac pink	554	96	1
Dark blue	820	134	1

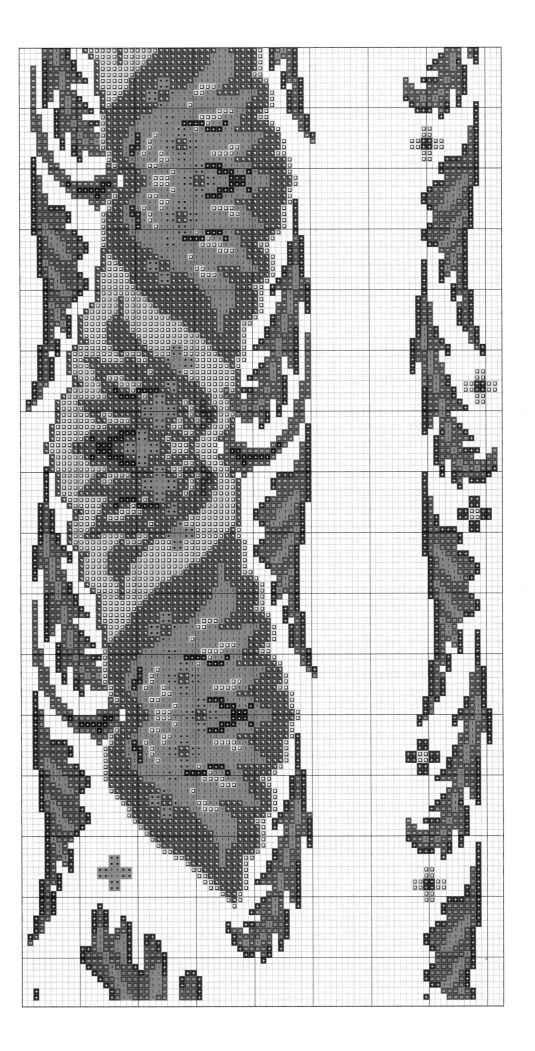

BOLSTER CUSHION

DMC

◥	798
☰	3814
▢	3756
▮	3766
✚	3765
▪	554
▪	820

·KLIMT·GOLD·AND· ·SPIRAL·DECORATION·

GUSTAV KLIMT, AN AUSTRIAN ARTIST, is a particular favourite of mine, so a cross stitch design inspired by his work had to be included in this book. Best known for his richly decorated, gold embellished pictures, I found many of the themes he chose were simply too big to be translated into cross stitch. So, ignoring such pieces as 'Judith', 'Salome' and 'The Kiss' (perhaps his best-known work), I chose instead his portrait of Adele Bloch-Bauer, a Viennese society lady.

In this picture the lady's head, shoulders and arms are painted in a naturalistic way, while the background, the armchair she is sitting on and the clothes she is wearing are all filled with flat pattern. One has to look hard to distinguish one object from another in the rich feast of decoration. The picture inspired me to create a mirror frame design: as almost all the picture is filled with pattern, cutting out a space for the mirror would not destroy its meaning. I used the spiralling pattern which decorates the armchair and the fluid pattern of the drapery round the body, which is scattered with rectangles of gold zig zag or spiral designs, inspired by Egyptian, Celtic, Byzantine and Japanese motifs. Taking some of the dominant pattern motifs from the portrait, I went on to produce three designs to decorate three different sized and shaped pot lids: a Celtic motif for the large oval lid, squares for the small round lid, and organic spirals for the large round lid.

Klimt often used spirals in his work, nowhere better than for the spiralling branches of his Tree of Life, a mural decoration designed for the Palais Stocklet in Brussels. The tree occupied an end wall, its coiling branches enveloping the room, extending along the side walls. The work was carried out in a mosaic of marble, inlaid with gold, metals, enamel and semi-precious stones, influenced by Klimt's visit to the mosaics of Ravenna. It was thinking of the marble and the copper of the Palais Stocklet Tree of Life mosaic that gave me the idea of combining these rich patterns with the smooth shine of the mirror and the shiny black glaze of the pots. ❦ ❦

A CONTEMPORARY OF KLIMT described his pattern as '...never ending, infinitely mutating primal matter - spinning, whirling, coiling, winding and twisting - a fiery whirlwind...' These qualities have inspired this unusual mirror frame and decorative pot lid collection.

·Spiralling·Mirror·Frame·

The overwhelming colouring of the portrait of Adele Bloch-Bauer, the original inspiration for this project, is gold, though there are touches of red to echo the mouth and skin tones, and of brown to act as a foil for the gold. To try to recreate Klimt's extraordinary palette, I have used metallic braids in five colours: a silvery gold, a gold, a red gold, a copper and a bronze. To create extra variety of colour and texture a range of stranded cottons is integrated into the design.

❦

DESIGN SIZE
8¼ x 14⅛in (21.5 x 37cm)

•

MATERIALS
• 15 x 22in (38 x 55cm) 14-count Aida in black
• Kreinik Fine (#8) Braid as listed in the key
• Stranded cottons as listed in the key
• Size 22 tapestry needle
• Black iron-on interfacing, same size as the Aida
• A1 sheet of black mount board
• Ruler and craft knife
• Double-sided adhesive tape
• PVA fabric glue
• 6 x 12in (15 x 30cm) mirror tile
• Corrugated cardboard
• 40in (1m) fine black cord (optional)
• 40in (1m) slightly thicker black cord (optional)
• Fabric to neaten back
• Needle and black thread for finishing
• 2 curtain rings and strong thread for hanging

❦

1   Mark the central horizontal and vertical guidelines on the fabric with tacking (see page 120). To help keep your place when stitching, continue to mark out the fabric into 20 block squares, starting from centre lines.

2   Follow the charts on pages 44 and 45. The embroidery is worked in both stranded cottons and metallic threads to give a variety of texture. The metallic threads act as highlights and give emphasis to the design. Use the metallic threads singly straight from the reel, in quite short lengths, approximately 20in (50cm). To avoid the

thread fraying, move the position of the needle on the thread from time to time. If the thread does start to fray, start a new length. When working with the stranded cottons, use two strands in the needle.

3   When the embroidery is complete, remove the guidelines and press (see page 121). Bond the black iron-on interfacing to the reverse of the embroidery following the manufacturer's instructions.

4   Cut a piece of black mount board to 8¼ x 14⅛in (21.5 x 37cm). Measure out the aperture carefully (see Fig 1) and cut out. With a black marker pen or a touch of black paint darken the white card revealed once the card is cut.

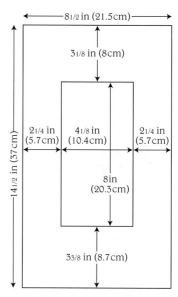

Fig 1 Size of card to support the embroidery.

5   Using the black side of the card as the back, apply strips of double-sided adhesive tape to the outer and inner edges of the top side of the card, pressing on firmly. Position the embroidery carefully on the card, so that the inner edge of the embroidery coincides with the cut out area. Starting with the inner adhesive tape, peel off the protective strips and press the embroidery in place. It is possible to lift and reposition it until you are satisfied.

6   Smooth the embroidery in place and attach to the outside strips of the double-sided adhesive tape.

7   In a calm frame of mind and with your sharpest scissors cut carefully into the centre of the fabric. Referring to Fig 2, cut a slit up the middle and then four diagonal cuts into the corners.

8   Fold the fabric through the aperture and stick it

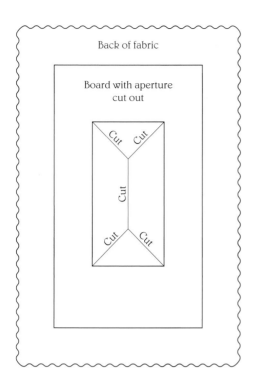

Fig 2 Back of embroidery fabric attached to the card by double-sided adhesive tape. Cut the centre as shown.

not be black). Position the mirror tile in the centre. Attach the four adhesive pads supplied with the tile in the corners.

10 To make an even surface cut strips of card to fit round the edges of the mirror. Stick these in place on the backing card, as shown in Fig 3. (Strips of corrugated card from a supermarket box are ideal for this because they are lightweight.)

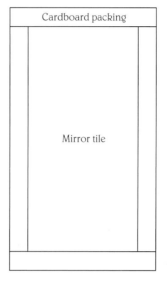

to the back of the board with PVA glue. Use the glue sparingly and avoid it getting too close to the aperture.

9 Cut another piece of card for the backing (this need

Fig 3 Backing board with mirror in position and border of card to make the surface level.

THIS TOP RIGHT CORNER of the mirror frame could be stitched to make a spectacle case or purse.

11 Place the embroidered frame over the inset mirror. Check that the corners look neat where they are reflected in the mirror. If you wish, you can add a fine black cord round the edge of the aperture held in place with invisible stitches into the folded edge of the embroidery. Glue the layers together.

12 Fold the surplus fabric round the back of the backing board. Fold and mitre the corners neatly (see page 124). Hold in place with double-sided adhesive tape or glue. If using glue, keep well away from the edges of the frame. Cut a piece of firm, dark fabric to the size of the backing board. Turn in the edges and stitch in place about 1/2in (1cm) in from the edge all round.

13 At this stage you might want to consider whether to add a further, thicker cord round the outside edge of the mirror frame.

14 On the back of the mirror frame, position two curtain rings at each side near to the top to take a suspension cord, or use a single ring in the centre. Stitch firmly in place to complete.

THESE STUNNING metallic braid lids will embellish storage pots of various sizes.

·Decorative·Pot·Lids·

These decorative lids, worked on a finer fabric than the mirror frame, use just three colours of fine metallic braid: a light gold, a red gold and a copper.

DESIGN SIZE
Large round: 3½in (8.8cm) diameter
Oval: 2.⅞in x 2in (7.3cm x 5cm)
Small round: 1¼in (3.2cm) diameter

•

MATERIALS (for all three pots)
• Small piece of black 18-count Aida
• Kreinik Very Fine (#4) Braid Gold 002, Aztec Gold 202HL and Copper 021, 1 spool of each
• Size 24 tapestry needle
• Iron-on interfacing, same size as the Aida
• Decorative pots (see Suppliers, page 126)

1 Follow the charts, right, and work all three designs on one piece of fabric, leaving a gap of at least an inch (2.5cm) between the designs, using a single thickness of Very Fine Braid. Use of a frame is not essential with pieces of this size, but mark the centre lines of each design on to your fabric before you begin.

2 When the embroidery is complete, press carefully (see page 121). Bond the iron-on interfacing to the reverse of the embroidery. Cut out the designs using the template supplied with the pots. Assemble according to the manufacturer's instructions

Variations

❦ You could use the mirror frame as a picture frame, perhaps for a certificate or precious document.

❦ Work just the top right hand corner of the mirror to make a spectacle case. With a black or gold cord stitched to it, it would make a stunning accessory to hang round the neck.

❦ The small round pot lid would make an ideal brooch.

LARGE ROUND POT LID

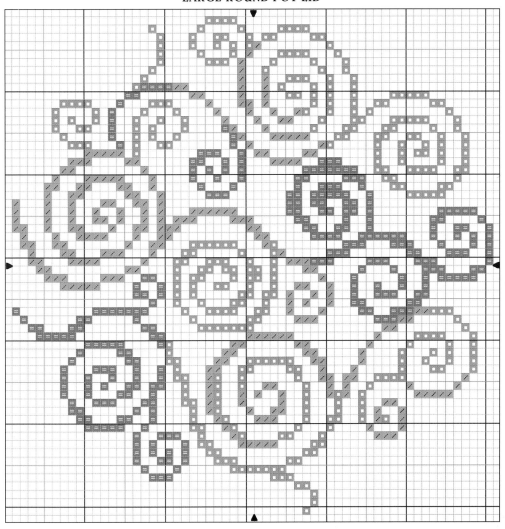

OVAL POT LID

SMALL ROUND POT LID

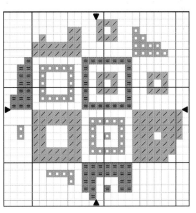

DECORATIVE POT LIDS

Kreinik Very Fine (#4) Braid

002 (#4) Gold

202HL (#4) Aztec Gold

021 (#4) Copper

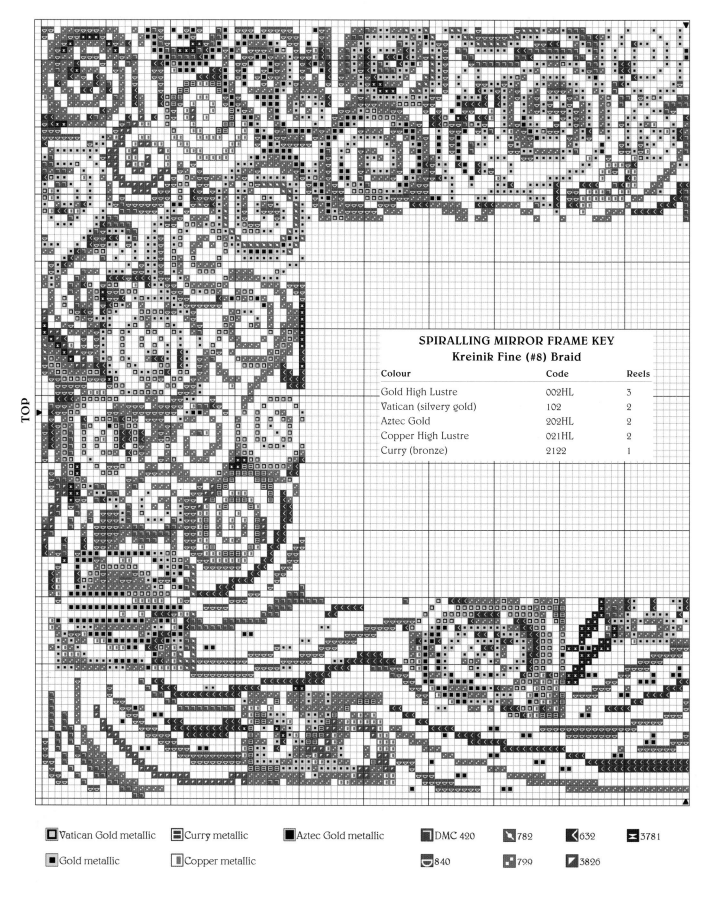

SPIRALLING MIRROR FRAME KEY
Kreinik Fine (#8) Braid

Colour	Code	Reels
Gold High Lustre	002HL	3
Vatican (silvery gold)	102	2
Aztec Gold	202HL	2
Copper High Lustre	021HL	2
Curry (bronze)	2122	1

Vatican Gold metallic   Curry metallic   Aztec Gold metallic   DMC 420   782   632   3781

Gold metallic   Copper metallic   840   799   3826

STRANDED COTTONS

Colour	DMC	Anchor	Madeira	Skeins
Hazel	420	375	2105	1
Aztec ochre	782	901	2213	1
Gold cotton	729	890	2009	2
Bright rust	3826	1049	2306	1
Dark copper	632	936	2304	1
Coffee	840	379	1912	1
Mocha brown	3781	1050	2003	1

BOTTOM

·ART·NOUVEAU·
·FLOWERS·

THESE FLORAL STUDIES of stylized iris, tulip and columbine are brought together as a series by the unifying border design used on each. The border is based on one used to advertise the new 'L' Art Nouveau' gallery which opened in Paris in 1895. The motifs at the corners are stylised plant forms, and the shallow, flattened curves with sudden, sharp angles are very characteristic of the Art Nouveau style. Long, thin proportion is typical of the period. There had been a tendency to elongate figures – Edward Burne-Jones' ladies were a good example. Aubrey Beardsley continued and exaggerated the trend, and other artists applied it to plant forms as well as to the human form. Japanese prints, so very influential on the art of the late nineteenth century, often came in extremely long, thin proportions – a novelty that artists and designers wanted to experiment with.

The iris was a favourite flower at the time. Its proportion and its strong, sculptural shapes appealed to designers. Its habit of growing near water was an added attraction. The curves and eddies of water and the long, sinuous curves of waterweed were ideal subjects for Art Nouveau artists. There was a vogue during this period for creating patterns from the most unlikely insects, but the most popular was the dragonfly, shown

PROPONENTS OF ART NOUVEAU found plants and insects a never-ending source of inpiration. Undulating lines and elongated proportions so typical of the style produce these delicate columbine, tulip and iris pictures.

here hovering over the iris. The inspiration for the iris design was a textile designed by Linsay P. Butterfield and woven by Alexander Morton & Co. around 1900. The original textile repeated groups of plants, but I have chosen just one here.

The tulip is also derived from a textile design. The original is printed on a dark navy cotton background and has an additional leaf, a large five-sided, waterlily leaf, behind the two flower heads. This is one of my favourite designs. The way the leaves curve and relate to the curves of the stems appeals to me very much. It is undoubtedly artificial and contrived but that, I feel, gives it its beauty.

The columbine, or aquilegia, design is based on a plate in Eugène Grasset's collection of plant studies, published as *La Plante et ses Applications Ornementales* in 1897. The columbine is an unusual and pretty flower with attractively shaped leaves. In the original it is shown in yellows against dark blue, but I chose the more naturalistic colours of mauvey pinks because they bring together the mauves of the iris and the pinks of the tulip.

·Iris·Tulip·and· ·Columbine·Pictures·

These floral pictures of columbine, tulip and iris, all elegant and curving in the typical Art Nouveau style, are easy to stitch using only cross stitch and back stitch and would make lovely gifts, either singly or as a set.

DESIGN SIZE
Each 4¼ x 9½in (11 x 24cm) approximately, for a frame or mount aperture of 5½ x 11in (14 x 28cm)
Stitch count: each 63 x 130

•

MATERIALS (for each design)
• 9½ x 16½in (24 x 42cm) 28-count Zweigart very pale blue Annabelle evenweave, colour 550 (or 27½ x 16½in (70 x 42cm) for all three designs)
• Stranded cottons as listed in each key

1   Mark the central horizontal and vertical guidelines on the fabric with tacking (see page 120). If you have chosen to use the evenweave fabric illustrated (a 28-count cotton, slightly slubbed to give a linen look) then use an embroidery frame for best results (see page 120).

If you prefer to work on Aida choose Fabric Flair 14-count Aida in snow blue, colour 550. For each design about half a skein of the dark smoky green 3768 will be needed and small amounts of the other colours.

2   Following the relevant chart on pages 49–51, work the design over two threads of the fabric, using two strands of stranded cotton for the cross stitch. Work the cross stitch first, leaving the back stitching detail until the end. If you want to start with the border, begin at the centre line and work outwards, counting carefully. When you begin the flower designs, start near to the centre guidelines so that you have a reference point to count from.

3   To work the back stitch in the tulip and columbine designs, use two strands. To work the back stitch in the iris design, use two strands for the flower. Instead of keeping to the vertical and horizontal, the lines stretch diagonally over longer distances, though try to avoid making a single stitch cover more than two squares on the chart. Using an evenweave will allow you to be more flexible with the placement of stitches. Outline the dragonfly wings in the dark blue used to outline the flower. The leading edges of the upper wings, between the dark pink cross stitches, is worked in two strands, the rest in one. All the lines inside the wings are worked with a single strand of the dark pink.

4   When all the embroidery is complete, remove the guidelines, press and frame (see page 123 for advice).

TULIP

DMC

Symbol	DMC
◸	3768
T	3817
◹	502
3	504
L	600
N	602
≫	604
∧	3689
II	738
·	B5200

Back Stitch in:
—— 3768

TULIP KEY

Colour	DMC	Anchor	Madeira
Dark smoky green	3768	851	1706
Light misty green	3817	875	1209
Medium misty green	502	876	1703
Very pale green	504	1042	1701
Dark pink	600	1006	0704
Vivid pink	602	63	0702
Sugar pink	604	55	0614
Pale pink	3689	49	0607
Light tan	738	942	2013
White	B5200	1	white

IRIS

DMC

◤	3768
T	3817
◣	502
+	341
∩	791
⊹	340
⊃	3746
L	600
=	3822
·	B5200

Back Stitch in:

———600

———791

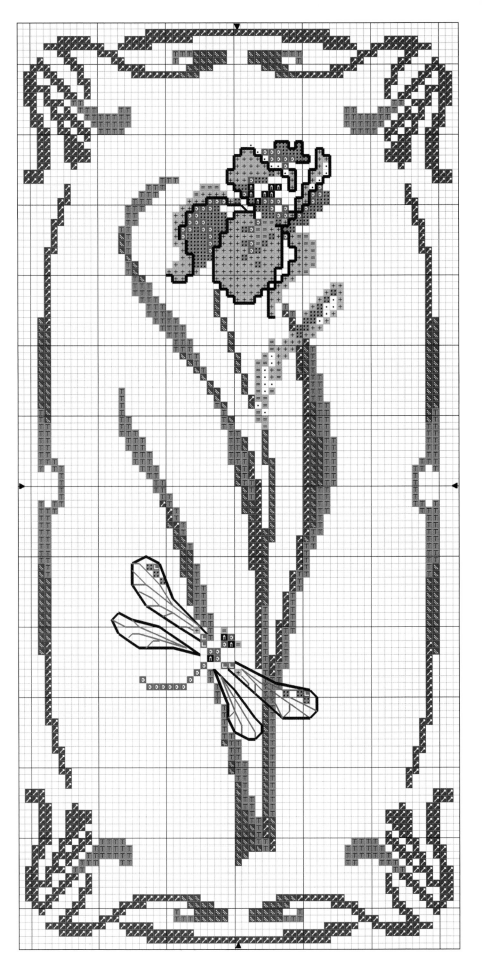

IRIS KEY

Colour	DMC	Anchor	Madeira
Dark smoky green	3768	851	1706
Light misty green	3817	875	1209
Medium misty green	502	876	1703
Light blue	341	117	0901
Dark blue	791	123	0904
Lavender	340	118	0902
Bright violet	3746	1030	0703
Dark Pink	600	1006	0704
Yellow	3822	305	0109
White	B5200	1	white

COLUMBINE

DMC

⬚	3768
⬚	3817
⬚	502
+	341
⬚	340
⬚	3746
⬚	3689
⬚	316
⬚	315
‖	738

Back Stitch in:

————791

————315

COLUMBINE KEY

Colour	DMC	Anchor	Madeira
Dark smoky green	3768	851	1706
Light misty green	3817	875	1209
Medium misty green	502	876	1703
Light blue	341	117	0901
Dark blue	791	123	0904
Lavender	340	118	0902
Bright violet	3746	1030	0703
Pale pink	3689	49	0607
Medium antique mauve	316	1017	0809
Dark antique mauve	315	1019	0810
Light tan	738	942	2013

51

·TIFFANY'S·DECORATIVE·GLASS·

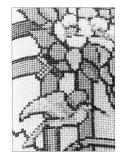

LOUIS COMFORT TIFFANY was one of the giants of the Art Nouveau period, a brilliant artist in coloured glass at the height of his creative powers around the turn of the century. He is remembered for his achievements in coloured glass windows, in his sinuous, iridescent, decorative vases and for his lamps that combined coloured glass shades with bronze or pottery sculptured bases. The projects in this chapter derive their inspiration from his decorative glass windows.

Born in 1848, Tiffany was the rich son of a family who owned the famous Tiffany and Co jewellery shops; consequently he grew up surrounded by *objets d'art* – by decorated Japanese fans and sun shades, prints, decorative metalwork, Islamic tiles and textiles and by creative craftsmen from a variety of disciplines. When he decided to become an artist he had money to study abroad and to travel widely, and when he devoted his energies to glass creations he could afford to employ experts from around the world.

Stained glass had seen a very strong revival during the second half of the nineteenth century, largely because of the rebirth of Gothic-style church building. Morris and Co created memorable windows from different coloured glass with details painted onto them. Tiffany wanted to create all his effects using the glass itself, with patterns being produced by the leading. In this he was inspired by the early examples he had seen at Chartres, and by Byzantine glass mosaics he had seen on his travels abroad. As the range of glass available commercially was inadequate he started to make his own, experimenting by adding various oxides and chemicals to his glass. By the 1890s he was a leading glass producer, his stock including a phenomenal 5,000 varieties of glass in a full range of colours and a variety of textures and degrees of translucency.

Movement and vitality were important aims in Art Nouveau and by exploiting the shifting light through his glass Tiffany achieved a constantly changing image. He wanted to capture the almost kaleidoscopic effect of varied reflections he had seen in the mosaics of the east. During the 1880s and 90s Tiffany developed many glassmaking techniques in order to create the

THIS WORK-BOX AND PINCUSHION use favourite motifs from the repertoire of American designer Louis Comfort Tiffany. Compare these with the reproduction on page 11, where Tiffany has used the same colour scheme and blossom in conjunction with a goldfish bowl circled by parrots.

effects he wanted. One of these was 'confetti' glass, where clear glass was poured over chips of coloured glass giving a fractured effect, very useful for capturing effects of light through foliage. Different textures were achieved by folding and manipulating the sheets of glass to give different intensity of colour. Different surface textures from his opalescent glass or his moulded glass 'jewels' which could create prismatic effects added to the vitality.

In translating his style into embroidery it is only possible to hint at the qualities light gives his glass. The work-box design of cherry blossom and birds against a bamboo trellis was based on Tiffany's designs in 1900 for the windows of a garden room. Its charm derives from the contrast between the verticals and horizontals of the bamboo and the organic patterns formed by the branches and leaves, which are accentuated by the black lines of the 'leading' which holds the mosaic of glass pieces in place. This design uses an irregularly coloured Rustico Aida to capture something of the variety of surface, while the lake landscape uses broken colour and a touch of metallic thread to hint at the same effect.

The lake landscape picture features some of Tiffany's favourite motifs. To translate the sort of composition designed for a large church or hotel window into a small cross stitch design necessitates some simplification. At this scale black leading lines tend to overwhelm the composition so to compensate in places they have been stitched in paler tones, and in others left out. Nevertheless I hope it retains the characteristic Tiffany colouring, something of the variety of reflectivity and instantly evokes the splendid windows which inspired it. ❦ ❦

·Bamboo·Blossom· ·and·Birds·Work-Box·

A dark oak work-box has been chosen to display this design. It is a traditional one with a sliding tray for storing small items and a padded top that allows it to double as a stool. In adapting the design for a padded work-box I included a piped edging which can accomodate to the curve of the pad. If it is to be displayed flat, a black edging line might be used to finish it off. The coloured, unstitched background is an important part of the design, allowing the embroidery to grow quite quickly.

DESIGN SIZE
14¼ x 11¼in (36 x 28.5cm) approximately
Stitch count: 205 x 160

•

MATERIALS
• 20 x 16in (50 x 40cm) 14-count green Rustico Aida
(Zweigart code 692)
• Stranded cottons as listed in the key
• Size 24 tapestry needle
• Dark oak work-box with padded lid (see Suppliers
page 126)
• Black piping or upholstery cord
• Fabric or stiff paper to back the work-box pad
• Staple gun or tacks (optional)

1   Mark the central horizontal and vertical guidelines on the fabric with tacking (see page 120).
2   Following the charts on pages 56 and 57, begin stitching the branches near the centre using two strands of stranded cotton. Use black to work the outlines, then fill in the coloured spaces with cross stitch.
3   When the embroidery is complete, press carefully (see page 121). Leave the tacking guidelines in for the moment to help position the embroidery over the work-box pad.
4   Stretch the embroidery over the pad and tack down according to the manufacturer's instructions, or stretch over the pad as you would over card for a picture using linen thread to secure it (see page 123). Remove the guidelines.

5 To finish, tack piping or upholstery cord with a tape edging to the edge of the pad so that it conceals the narrow gap and provides a black outline for the design.

6 Assemble in the work-box lid according to the manufacturer's instructions, with the stiff paper or fabric concealing the underside.

·Blossom·Pincushion·

 This pincushion features a small spray of flowers with leaves, mounted in a dark wood pincushion with a simple turned decoration. The design could be used on any small item, or you could embroider one or two of the birds from the work-box chart on page 56 and make a matching needlecase.

DESIGN SIZE
2¼ x 2¼in (5.5 x 5.5cm)
Stitch count: 31 x 32

•

MATERIALS
• 6 x 6in (15 x 15cm) 14-count Rustico Aida in green
(Zweigart code 692)
• Stranded cottons as listed in the key
• Size 24 tapestry needle
• 3½in (9cm) diameter wooden base pincushion
(see Suppliers page 126)

•

1 Follow the chart and work the design using two strands of stranded cotton and cross stitch.

2 When the embroidery is complete, place the fabric over the pincushion pad and secure it with a few pins near the base. Fasten it to the bottom of the pad with a few staples. Alternatively, you could run a gathering stitch around about ½in (1.25cm) in from the edge, pulling the thread tight and fastening off.

3 Trim the edges of the embroidered fabric so that there is room for the securing screw, then assemble according to the manufacturer's instructions.

Variations
• The work-box shown can accommodate a design stitched with tapestry wools as well as stranded cottons, so you could substitute harder-wearing wools on 14-count canvas.

• The bamboo, blossom and birds design could be framed as a picture or worked as a cushion instead of being mounted in a work-box in which case a black line should be worked in cross stitch around the edge to replace the black cord edging.

WORK-BOX AND PINCUSHION KEY

Colour	DMC	Anchor	Madeira	Skeins
Black	310	403	black	3
White	B5200	1	white	1
Christmas green	702	257	1306	1
Dark bay leaf green	319	218	1313	1
Medium green	987	210	1407	1
Light emerald green	913	204	1212	1
Mid emerald green	911	227	1301	1
Very light jade	564	206	1208	1
Mid jade	562	208	1213	1
Very dark jade	561	212	1205	1
Pale lime ice	472	253	1414	1
Light lime	3819	279	1610	1
Lime green	907	255	1410	1
Yellow beige	3047	842	2205	1
Salmon pink	760	1022	0405	1
Electric blue	996	433	1103	1

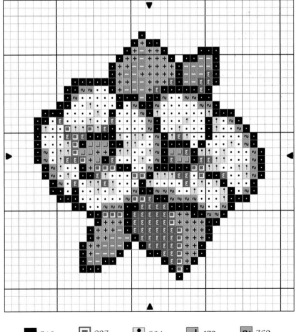

■ 310	▣ 987	⬆ 564	⌐ 472	∿ 760
• B5200	▬ 913	Ɛ 562	+ 3819	

BAMBOO, BLOSSOM AND BIRDS WORK-BOX

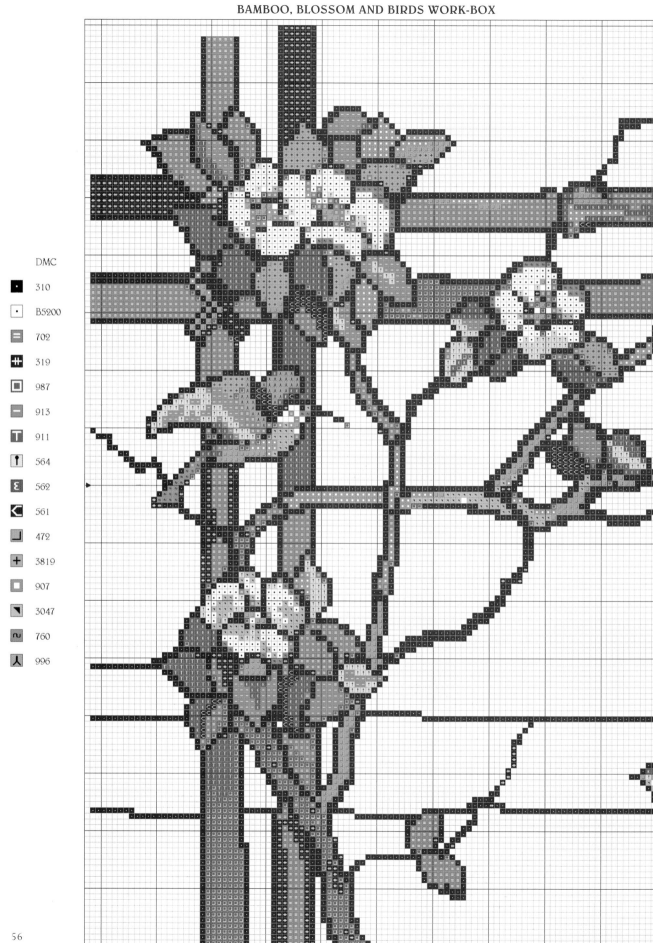

DMC	
■	310
·	B5200
≡	702
⊞	319
▣	987
−	913
T	911
!	564
Ɛ	562
◀	561
⌐	472
+	3819
▢	907
◥	3047
∾	760
人	996

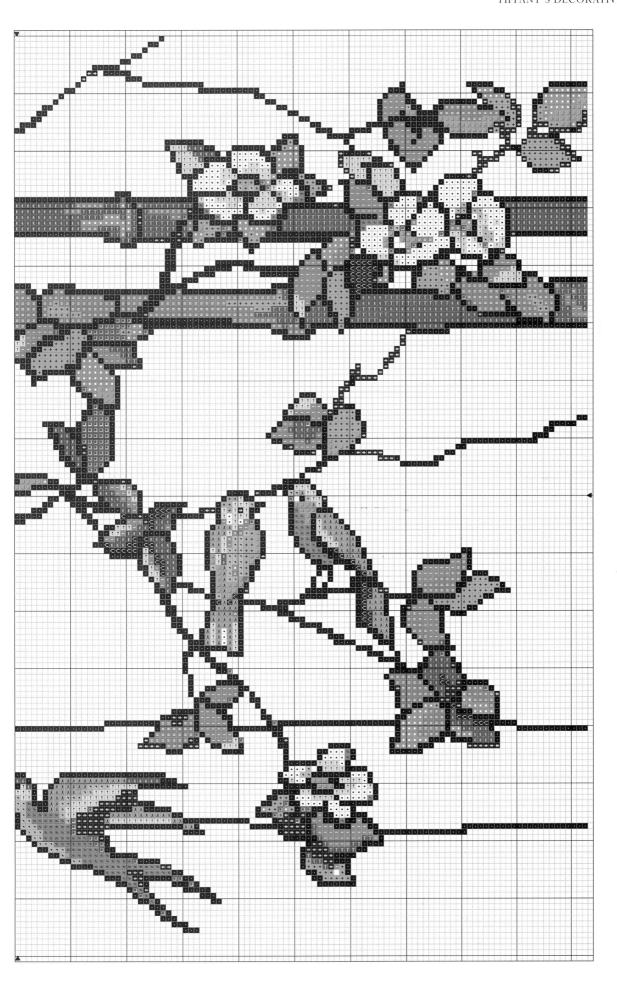

·Lake·Landscape·Picture·

his idyllic landscape seen on a summer's day features some of Tiffany's favourite motifs. A pillared terrace, covered by the coiling stems and swaying flowers of a wisteria, frames a view across water to a distant mountain. Close to the terrace are water lilies and irises, whilst further out a yacht approaches. All the elements are used for their decorative and ornamental qualities, emphasised by the pattern of the leaded lines.

❦

DESIGN SIZE
6½ x 11⅛in (17 x 29cm) approximately
Stitch count: 95 x 160

•

MATERIALS
• 12 x 18in (30 x 45cm) Fabric Flair 14-count Aida in snow blue (code 550)
• Stranded cottons as listed in the key
• Kreinik metallic threads as listed in the key
• Size 24 tapestry needle

❦

1   Mark the central horizontal and vertical guidelines on the fabric with tacking (see page 120).

2   Following the charts on pages 60 and 61, use two strands of stranded cotton for the cross stitch and one strand for the back stitch. Begin stitching near the centre, perhaps with the black hull of the yacht. From there you could work the shoreline of the far side and then the black lines defining the edges of the foreground columns, to provide a framework for the remaining stitching. Metallic blending filament has been used with the very pale blue for highlights on the water but if you prefer you could work those stitches with stranded cotton alone. A purple blending filament added to the two blue violet colours of the wisteria flowers in the illustration could be omitted.

3   When the embroidery is complete, remove the guidelines and press gently (see page 121). Mount and frame the design in your chosen frame (see page 123).

LAKE LANDSCAPE KEY

Colour	DMC	Anchor	Madeira	Skeins
Black	310	403	black	1
White	B5200	1	white	1
Lake blue	519	1038	1105	1
Dark lake blue	518	1039	1106	1
Ecrut	ecrut	926	ecrut	1
Light tan	738	942	2013	1
Orange	977	1002	2307	1
Dark rust	720	326	0309	1
Brown	640	903	1905	1
Dark green	991	189	1204	1
Green	989	261	1401	1
Misty green	3815	877	1205	1
Light sea foam green	3813	1042	1701	1
Lime green	907	255	1410	1
Very pale blue	3756	1037	1104	1
Grey blue	931	1034	1711	1
Very dark blue	791	123	0904	1
Bright blue	798	137	0911	1
Light cornflower blue	794	175	0907	1
Dark blue violet	3746	1030	0903	1
Mid blue violet	340	118	0902	1
Pale lavender	211	342	0801	1
Buttercup yellow	743	305	0113	1
Dandelion yellow	727	293	0110	1

Kreinik blending filament

Baby blue	9400BF			1 reel
Purple	012BF			1 reel

A DAYDREAM LANDSCAPE composed of favourite themes from Tiffany's studio. A perfect day seen from the security of a wisteria-covered terrace, looking out over sunlit water to the wild mountains beyond. The little yacht brings promise of a visitor from the outside world.

DMC		
◐	720	
⦂	727	
■	640	
Y	3815	
✕	743	
·	B5200	
◇	3756	
/	211	
⊿	977	
◥	518	
⬚	907	
◖	3746	
⊠	504	
▥	798	
H	794	
◪	791	
◣	738	
Z	951	
▮	991	
✕	Ecru	
⩚	519	
■	310	
◪	340	
▬	989	

Back Stitch in:
——— 310

NOTE ▶

Use Baby blue Blending Filament 9400BF with 3756. Add Purple Blending Filament 012BF to 3746 and 340 when stitching the flowers

·WALTER·CRANE'S· ·FLOWER·LADIES·

THE INSPIRATION for these three designs is a series of decorative tiles designed by Walter Crane in 1902. Walter Crane was one of the foremost illustrators of the late nineteenth century, specialising in books for children. He was a versatile artist designing for many media including books, printed fabric, carpets, wallpaper and ceramics. A favourite theme of Crane's, epitomising Art Nouveau, was the association of women and flowers. Often they become the flowers, otherwise they carry armfuls of lilies or wear blossoms in their hair. In these three pictures each lady is the spirit, the personification of the flower. Their figures take on something of the organic energy of the plant forms, accommodating to the sinuous curves of natural growth. For each design, I have chosen a different coloured background to accentuate the largely monochrome colouring that is typical of each flower. ❦ ❦

THESE PICTURES, inspired by the work of Walter Crane, bring together two of the favourite themes of the turn of the century - beautiful women and flowers. These are the antecedents of Cicely Mary Barker's Flower Fairies.

·The·Daffodil·Lady·

The Daffodil Lady is fresh and sharp in spring yellows and greens. Her clothes, like the petals of the daffodils, are tattered and swirled by the fresh breeze. The design would be suitable for a 12 x 12in (30 x 30cm) picture frame.

THE DAFFODIL LADY

DMC

◤	445	✚	741
✕	307	G	472
₪	444	⏛	3819
⋀	727	◪	580
◩	725	✚	3046
·	B5200	▯	832
⦂	746	◉	831
◇	781	━	898
Z	972		

Back Stitch in:
———831

THE DAFFODIL LADY KEY

Colour	DMC	Anchor	Madeira	Skeins
Lemon	445	288	0103	2
Mid lemon	307	290	0104	1
Dark lemon	444	297	0106	1
Very light topaz	727	293	0110	1
Mid topaz	725	306	0113	2
White	B5200	1	white	1
Off-white	746	386	0101	1
Burnt orange	781	308	2213	1
Golden orange	972	298	0107	1
Orange	741	314	0201	1
Lightest green	472	264	1409	1
Yellow green	3819	279	609	1
Dark green	580	281	1608	1
Beige	3046	887	2206	1
Golden khaki	832	907	2202	1
Khaki	831	277	2201	1
Brown	898	360	2006	1

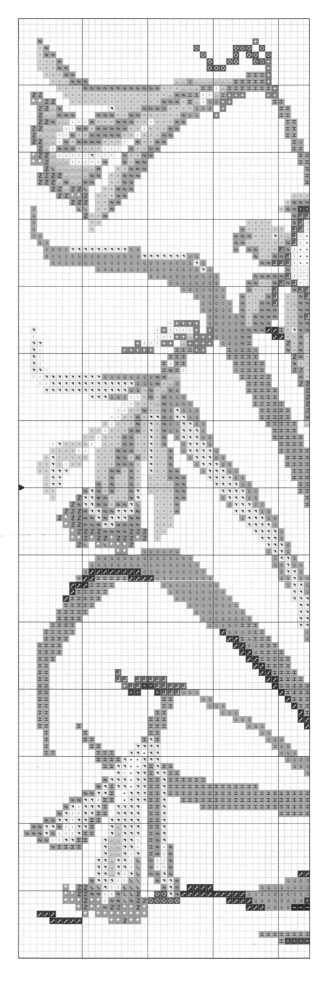

·The·Poppy·Lady·

The Poppy Lady is warm and sensuous, representing the hot colours of a midsummer cornfield and hinting at lazy afternoons dreaming in the sun. Morpheus, bringer of dreams, is symbolised by the poppy. The design is suitable for a 12 x 12in (30 x 30cm) picture frame.

THE POPPY LADY
DMC

R	606	3	3821
I	321	Y	353
X	350	+	3341
Z	758	X	3825
U	356	Z	922
⊿	355	■	920
·	B5200	▶	977
/	746	(	898
⋀	951		

Back Stitch in:

————355

THE POPPY LADY KEY

Colour	DMC	Anchor	Madeira	Skeins
Red	606	334	0209	1
Christmas red	321	47	0510	1
Coral	350	11	0213	1
Light terracotta	758	882	0403	1
Mid terracotta	356	1013	0402	1
Dark terracotta	355	1014	0401	1
White	B5200	1	white	1
Off-white	746	386	0101	1
Flesh	951	1009	2308	1
Corn	3821	891	2208	1
Peachy pink	353	6	0504	1
Peach	3341	382	0302	1
Apricot	3825	1047	2313	1
Light copper	922	1003	0311	1
Copper	920	1004	0312	1
Golden brown	977	1002	2307	1
Dark brown	898	360	2006	1

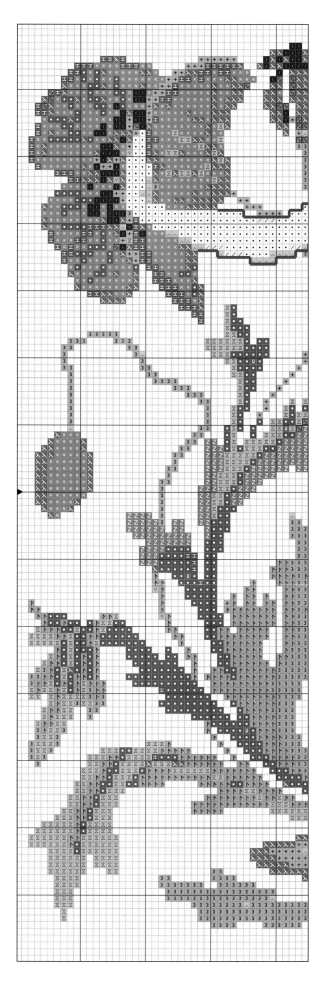

·The·Anemone·Lady·

The Anemone Lady is vivacious and pretty in vibrant pinks and mauves, set off by her stamen black hair. The design is suitable for a 12 x 12in (30 x 30cm) picture frame.

THE ANEMONE LADY

DMC

■	310	◇	892
人	3354	+	948
·	B5200	⌐	208
↑	917	\	211
◣	333	♥	554
C	309	↓	3607
▬	550	m	340
◪	792	Back Stitch in:	
I	3747	————917	

THE ANEMONE LADY KEY

Colour	DMC	Anchor	Madeira	Skeins
White	B5200	1	white	2
Black	310	403	black	1
Flesh	948	1011	0306	1
Dusty rose	3354	74	0606	1
Vivid geranium pink	892	28	0412	1
Crimson pink	309	39	0507	1
Fuchsia mauve	3607	87	0708	1
Dark fuchsia mauve	917	89	0705	1
Light violet pink	554	96	0711	1
Light violet	211	342	0801	1
Mid violet	208	111	0804	1
Dark violet	550	102	0714	1
Light lavender blue	3747	117	0907	1
Mid lavender blue	340	118	0902	2
Dark lavender blue	333	119	0903	1
Cornflower blue	792	178	0905	1

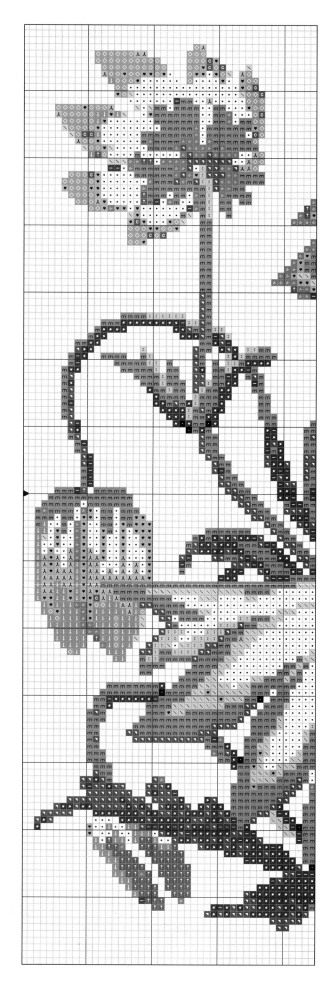

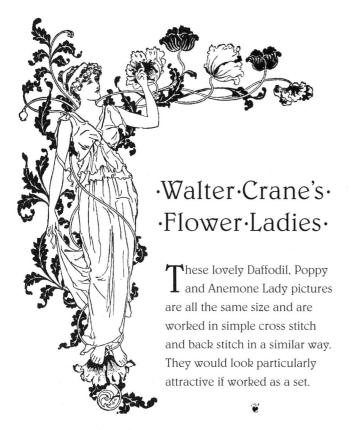

·Walter·Crane's· ·Flower·Ladies·

These lovely Daffodil, Poppy and Anemone Lady pictures are all the same size and are worked in simple cross stitch and back stitch in a similar way. They would look particularly attractive if worked as a set.

❦

DESIGN SIZE FOR EACH PICTURE
10 x 10in (25.5 x 25.5cm)
Stitch count: 140 x 140

•

MATERIALS
FOR THE DAFFODIL LADY
• 18 x 18in (46 x 46cm) square of 14-count Zweigart Aida in primrose yellow (code 2)
• Stranded cottons as listed in the key on page 64
• Size 24 tapestry needle

FOR THE POPPY LADY
• 18 x 18in (46 x 46cm) square of 14-count Zweigart Aida in peach pink (code 302)
• Stranded cottons as listed in the key on page 66
• Size 24 tapestry needle

FOR THE ANEMONE LADY
• 18 x 18in (46 x 46cm) square of 14-count Zweigart Aida in blush pink (code 400)
• Stranded cottons as listed in the key on page 68
• Size 24 tapestry needle

❦

1   Select the correctly coloured square of Aida for the picture you wish to work and begin by marking the central vertical and horizontal guidelines with tacking (see page 120).

2   Work each design following the relevant chart (Daffodil Lady on page 64/65, Poppy Lady on page 66/67 and Anemone Lady on page 68/69). Use two strands of stranded cotton for all the cross stitch throughout. For the back stitch use two strands on the Daffodil Lady and Anemone Lady and one strand on the Poppy Lady.

3   Begin by stitching the figure from the centre point outwards as this will provide lots of reference points to count from for placing flowers and leaves. The face and neck will only take shape when the back stitch is added. When the figure is complete, embroider the flowers, leaves and stems.

4   When all the stitching is complete remove the tacking guidelines and press (see page 121), then mount and frame (see page 123).

Variations

❦   The fabrics used are available in different counts so you could work the designs larger or smaller.

❦   You may want to stitch all three flower pictures on the same coloured background, in which case a white or cream would be a good choice. The predominant colour could then be picked up in a mount.

❦   You could work a single bud or flower head.

·LANDSCAPE·AS·DECORATION·

CHARLES ANNESLEY VOYSEY was a successful British Arts and Crafts architect who, in the spirit of the times, designed houses, furniture, household goods and lots of fabrics, wallpaper and carpets. His textile designs are instantly recognisable from his use of flat, unbroken colour bounded by a contrasting outline, a style which lends itself well to cross stitch design. It was a style that proved to be inspirational and was particularly admired by continental Art Nouveau designers, though he himself disliked the label Art Nouveau and claimed to prefer the absence of all ornament, something he aspired to in the houses he designed.

The inspiration for this charming clock came from a fabric design by Charles Annesley Voysey dating from 1896, showing a peaceful landscape scene, with a flock of birds and water seen through cypress and fruit trees. These were some of his favourite motifs and he often used them for his wallpaper and fabric designs.

Clocks were available in a fantastic range of styles around the turn of the century and some of the most desirable were the silver and enamel ones produced by Liberty. These, however, are quite sculptural and not suitable for cross stitch but they made me think about a clock as an art object rather than as a purely functional thing. Today we have digital clocks built into almost all electrical appliances but clocks with hands are far more satisfying and perhaps it is time to make them into decorative objects again.

Many of the clocks I looked at treated the numbers as part of the sculptural decoration or replaced them with words, such as 'Tempus fugit' (time flies), a Latin message most of us know too well; likewise the message 'Time and tide wait for no man' which Voysey used on one of the painted clocks he made for his own home. I felt much happier with the simple phrase 'Time enough' from a clock case by Archibald Knox, designer of many of the silver and pewter Liberty clocks. ❦ ❦

·Voysey·Landscape· ·Clock·

 This project, inspired by a Voysey woven fabric suggested itself for a clock design, since the large tree in the centre was ideally placed and almost round. I felt the twelve leaves on the inner edge were sufficient guide to the hours and the fruits to the quarters. The circling birds, watching stags and gliding swans gave a stillness and tranquillity to Voysey's design which suited the 'Time enough' motif. Using an embroidery frame is recommended for this design because working solid areas of colour can distort the fabric.

❧

DESIGN SIZE
9½ x 15¼in (24 x 39cm) approximately
Stitch count: 169 x 274

•

MATERIALS
- 19 x 23½in (48 x 60cm) 18-count Cadet Blue Aida, Zweigart (code 510)
- Stranded cottons as listed in the key
- Size 24 tapestry needle
- Iron-on interfacing 2⅛in (6cm) diameter circle
- Board or stiff card 12¼ x 18½in (31.5 x 47cm)
- Quartz clock movement and 40mm clock hands (see Suppliers page 126)
- Suitable sized mount with a semicircular head in a dark blue/green
- Picture frame 12¼ x 18½in (31.5 x 47cm)

❧

1   Mark the central horizontal and vertical guidelines on the fabric with tacking (see page 120).

2   Follow the chart on pages 74–75 and begin stitching near the centre using two strands of stranded cotton, working the cross stitch outlines first.

3   When the embroidery is complete, remove any tacking guidelines and iron the interfacing on the back to cover the centre of the clock face and reinforce the area. Make a hole for the spindle in the exact centre of the face.

4   Stretch the embroidered fabric over the piece of board or stiff card (see page 123). Make up as you would

a picture but bore a small hole right through the backing board so that the clock movement can be placed on the back of the picture. Place the spindle through the backing and the card with the embroidery mounted on it. Add the hands and securing nut and tighten.

5   To finish, chose a mount card and get your picture framer to cut a semicircular head. This should begin on a level with the top of the clock face's top leaf. Assemble the embroidered clock, the mount and the frame (see page 123 for framing advice). If using glass, insert a narrow strip of cardboard round the edges to prevent the glass from touching the clock hands.

Variations

❧   Individual motifs from this clock design could easily be used alone for cards or other small projects.

❧   The design could be adapted to an appliqué design, using machine stitching for the outlines.

❧   The clock face alone could be stitched for one of Framecraft's round or square clock kits, which include 14-count fabric.

❧   The blue birds of happiness could be stitched with a good luck message of your choice.

❧   Chose one of the fruit trees and stitch a decorative pot to cover the bottom third of the trunk.

VOYSEY LANDSCAPE CLOCK KEY

Colour	DMC	Anchor	Madeira	Skeins
Dark green	991	189	1204	3
Blue	518	1039	1106	2
Misty green	3816	876	1207	2
Orange	722	323	0307	1
Clear yellow	676	891	2208	1
Golden yellow	3827	323	0307	1
White	blanc	1	white	1
Tree trunk green	992	186	1202	1

SILHOUETTED TREES and simple plant, animal and bird shapes were hallmarks of the style of Charles Annesley Voysey.

DMC
991
518
3816
792
676
3887
BLANC
992

·PATTERNS·FROM·FLORAL·FOLIOS·

Late in the nineteenth century various artists published folios of coloured patterns and designs, including Eugène Grasset, Alphonse Mucha and Seguy. These contained decorative treatments of plants with suggestions for their use as borders, stained glass panels, book covers and wallpapers. The inspiration for the snowdrop bed linen designs came from Eugene Grasset's book of floral designs, *La Plante et ses Applications Ornementales*, originally published in 1897. He was a talented designer and illustrator and a major interpreter of Art Nouveau design. Both he and his English contemporary, Walter Crane, emphasised the importance of line and the stylisation of natural forms and acknowledged the influence of Japanese art.

For Grasset the starting point was nature itself and his floral designs lend themselves well to cross stitch interpretations, including his variations of ivy, dandelion, gourd, iris, monks hood and nasturtium. His two pages of snowdrop designs provided a source for the border pattern and for the snowdrop group at the centre of the cushion. This was isolated from an all-over design intended for a fabric or wallpaper. The original design is printed on a tan/orange background with the flowers in turquoise. I wanted more realistic white flowers and just outlining the petals gave the most effective result. Using lavender retained the delicacy of the flowers, whilst being strong enough to compete with the cross stitched leaves and stems. These delicate designs in peach and lavender will complement a wide range of bedroom decor. ❧ ❧

MANY ART NOUVEAU DESIGNS contain floral elements stylised to become part of the decorative structure. Here, the simple snowdrop, adapted from the right-hand border of the Grasset folio pictured above, forms the basis of a charming design on bed linen.

·Snowdrop·Pillow·Band·

he delicate pillow band is worked on white Aida band with a self-coloured picot edging. Charts are supplied for a left-hand and right-hand edge. If you wish, a matching border could be worked for the edge of a sheet.

❦

DESIGN SIZE
Each band 18¼ x 2in (47 x 5cm) approximately
Stitch count: 26 x 286

•

MATERIALS
• 20in (50cm) x 2in (5cm) wide white Aida band
(Zweigart code 7107). If you prefer linen, choose a 3in
(7.5cm) linen band with a drawn thread look edge
(Zweigart code 7272, colour 11) which is sufficient for
twenty-six stitches worked over two threads
• Stranded cottons as listed in the key
• Size 24 tapestry needle
• Peach-coloured pillow slip

❦

1 The design extends almost to the ends of the band so neaten the cut edges with a machine zigzag stitch or some hand-sewing, then fold the band in half lengthways and mark the centre.

2 Follow the chart below and on page 79, starting from the centre. The charts show two borders – one for a left-hand pillowcase and one for a right-hand. Work the cross stitch first using two strands of stranded cotton. Work the back stitch detail last using two strands. Work eight complete repeats and then continue the lines of peach and lavender until the embroidered part is the same size as the pillow slip you have selected. For two pillow bands you will need one skein each of sage green, emerald green, peach and lavender.

3 When complete, press the band (see page 121).

4 Turn the pillowslip inside out and unpick the seam on either side, from about 1–4in (2.5–10cm) from the opening edge. Turn the case to the right side and place the band in position about 1¼in (3cm) from the edge of the pillowslip. Pin in place and tuck the ends into the open seams. Using white sewing thread and hand or machine stitching, stitch the band in place along both edges, just inside the picot edging. Remove the pins. Turn inside out and restitch the seams to complete.

SNOWDROP PILLOW BAND

DMC				Back Stitch in:
▬ 581	◩ 913	Y 3824	☐ 340	———340

LEFT

RIGHT

·Snowdrop·Cushion·

This pretty cushion, worked on clean white Aida, is edged with peach piping to echo the peach of the pillowslip. The border is the same as that used for the left-hand edge of the pillow band, except for a slight variation in the lines along the edges. Notice the way a straight border has been used to create a square (see page 112 for more on Borders).

DESIGN SIZE
11½ x 11⅛in (29 x 29cm), made up as a 13⅛ x 13⅛in
(34 x 34cm) cushion
Stitch count: 162 x 162

•

MATERIALS
• 16 x 16in (41 x 41cm) 14-count Aida in white
(or a 28-count white Quaker Cloth or a linen-look
cotton evenweave)
• Stranded cottons as listed in the key
• Size 24 tapestry needle
• Backing fabric 16 x 18in (41 x 46cm)
• Piping cord covered with a peach cotton fabric
55in (140cm)
• Cushion pad 14 x 14in (36 x 36cm)

•

DETAIL of the Snowdrop Cushion's pretty central motif.

PILLOW BAND AND CUSHION KEY

Colour	DMC	Anchor	Madeira
Sage green	581	280	1609
Emerald green	913	204	1212
Peach	3824	8	0304
Lavender	340	118	0902
Light tan	676	891	2208

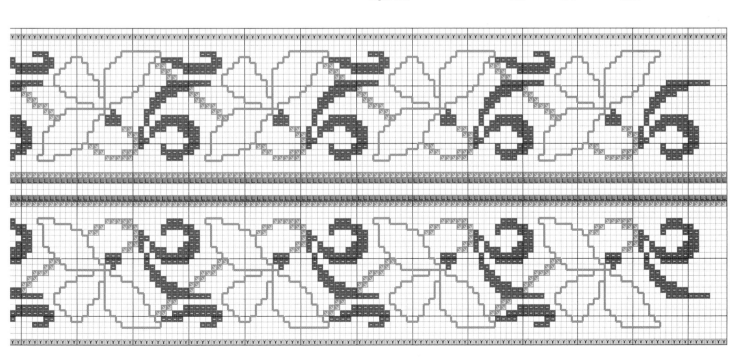

1 Mark the central horizontal and vertical guidelines on the fabric with tacking (see page 120).

2 Using two strands of stranded cotton for the cross stitch and the back stitch, follow the chart and work the design from the centre outwards. Avoid carrying threads across areas to be left white or they may show through: either finish off and start again or thread the cotton through other stitches on the back. For the cushion you will need two skeins of sage green and one each of the others listed.

3 When working the border, four repeats of the snowdrop lie along the right-hand edge of the cushion, from the bottom of the central square to the top of the outer square. The design is then turned through 90 degrees to fill the space along to the top left-hand corner. That process is repeated to complete the border. At the top of the fourth repeat the beginning of the next snowdrop has been left out and the bottom of the right-angled border has been allowed to overhang by a few squares for continuity.

4 When the embroidery is complete, remove the tacking guidelines and press (see page 121).

5 Make up the cushion back – see page 124 for instructions. As you may want to wash the cover it is best to make one with an easy opening.

Variations

❦ The central snowdrop group could be embroidered without the ferny leaves to fit into a circular mount, or be used as a dressing table mat with a lace edging, or to decorate a nightdress case.

❦ You could use some of the other Grasset floral patterns in the Small Motif section (page 104) and the Borders section (page 112) to create other linen bands and cushions.

SNOWDROP CUSHION

DMC

	DMC
▬	581
◸	913
Y	3824
L	340
+	676

Back Stitch in:
——340

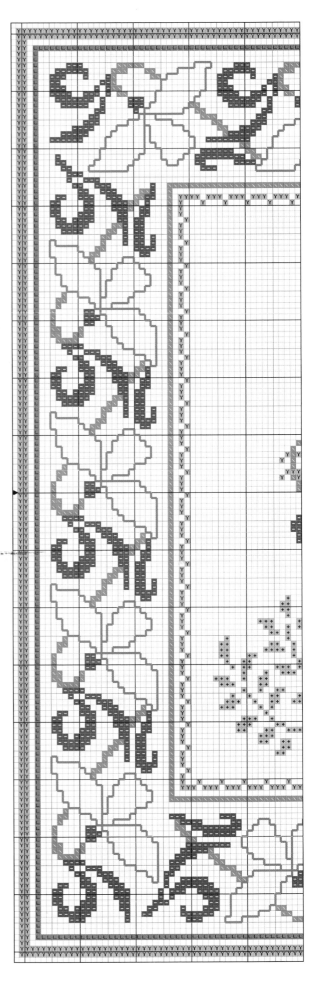

·THE·MACKINTOSH·ROSE·

THE CROSS STITCH DESIGNS in this section all feature the familiar stylised rose which came to be identified with the Glasgow School artists centred around Charles Rennie Mackintosh and the Glasgow School of Art.

The rose is such a well-known image that just a few visual cues let us identify it. Essentially it is a circle divided by dark lines representing petals. Mackintosh chose the rose as the decorative theme for his interior designs. Being such a simple shape it worked as stencil decoration on fabrics and walls and in the medium of stained glass. Other Glasgow artists used it in book illustration, furniture, jewellery and embroidery.

The strong rose pink was a keynote colour for Mackintosh's interior designs, the field for which he is best remembered now. He was a brilliant and innovative architect, but only received a handful of commissions, most famously the present Glasgow School of Art. His interiors were equally avant-garde. A typical room would have white walls and white carpet. There would only be a few pieces of furniture and these would be tall and narrow, painted white with sparing touches of pink and sometimes lilac, grey and silver. The whole space made a unified statement.

The designs in this section are all inspired by

Mackintosh's work. There are two cushions, a rose lady picture, a clock and a picture featuring a quotation from Mackintosh. They mostly share a palette of greys and pinks on pale neutral backgrounds and would best complement a simple, restrained setting, even perhaps a high-tech functional space.

The two rose cushions are variations on a theme and are based on drawings Mackintosh submitted for an international competition to design a 'House for an Art Lover', in 1901. These designs decorated a fitted wardrobe with typically long, thin doors, each with an inset square rose design near the top. Because he liked to juxtapose geometric with organic shapes I have added his well-known pattern of squares, used in other parts of his submission.

The rose lady picture was inspired by a stained glass panel. This lovely decoration has long appealed to me. The forms are considerably abstracted, turned into flat patterns. His style at this time grew out of the paintings he and his friends did in the 1890s. They were strongly influenced by the Symbolist movement and their works were characterised by attenuated human figures which seem to merge with and grow out of plant and tree forms.

The rose clock was inspired by the variety and

A CENTURY LATER the flower of Mackintosh's art continues to inspire and still looks contemporary. Here it has been used to create two rose cushions in pinks and greys and a rose lady picture based on a stained glass panel.

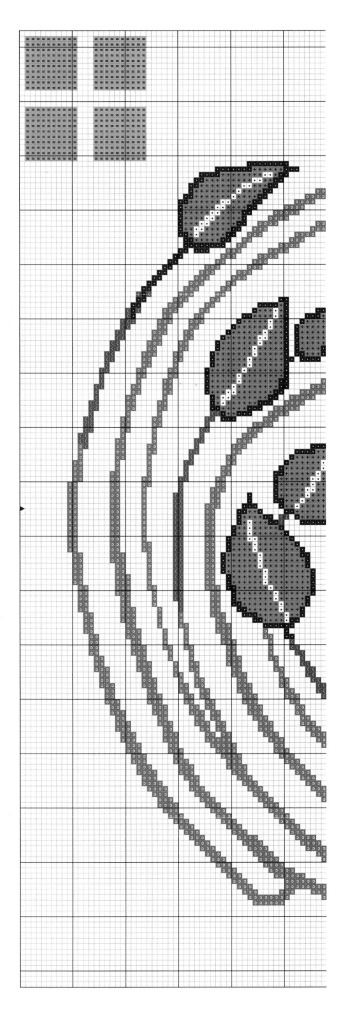

THE CROSS STITCH DESIGNS in this section all feature the familiar stylised rose which came to be identified with the Glasgow School artists centred around Charles Rennie Mackintosh and the Glasgow School of Art.

The rose is such a well-known image that just a few visual cues let us identify it. Essentially it is a circle divided by dark lines representing petals. Mackintosh chose the rose as the decorative theme for his interior designs. Being such a simple shape it worked as stencil decoration on fabrics and walls and in the medium of stained glass. Other Glasgow artists used it in book illustration, furniture, jewellery and embroidery.

The strong rose pink was a keynote colour for Mackintosh's interior designs, the field for which he is best remembered now. He was a brilliant and innovative architect, but only received a handful of commissions, most famously the present Glasgow School of Art. His interiors were equally

ROSE CUSHION KEY

Colour	DMC	Anchor	Madeira	Skeins (for 1 cushion)
Dark grey	413	236	1713	2
Mid grey	414	235	1801	1
Silver grey	318	399	1802	2
Dark plum	3803	69	0602	1
Mid plum	3687	68	0604	1
Light plum	3688	1016	0605	1
Pale sugar pink	3689	49	0607	1
Violet pink	554	96	0711	1
Lavender	211	342	0801	1
Misty green	3817	875	1209	1
White	B5200	1	white	1

DMC

◙	413	Ɛ	3803	人	3689	+	3817
K	414	Z	3687	=	554	·	B5200
Ɔ	318	✦	3688	N	211		

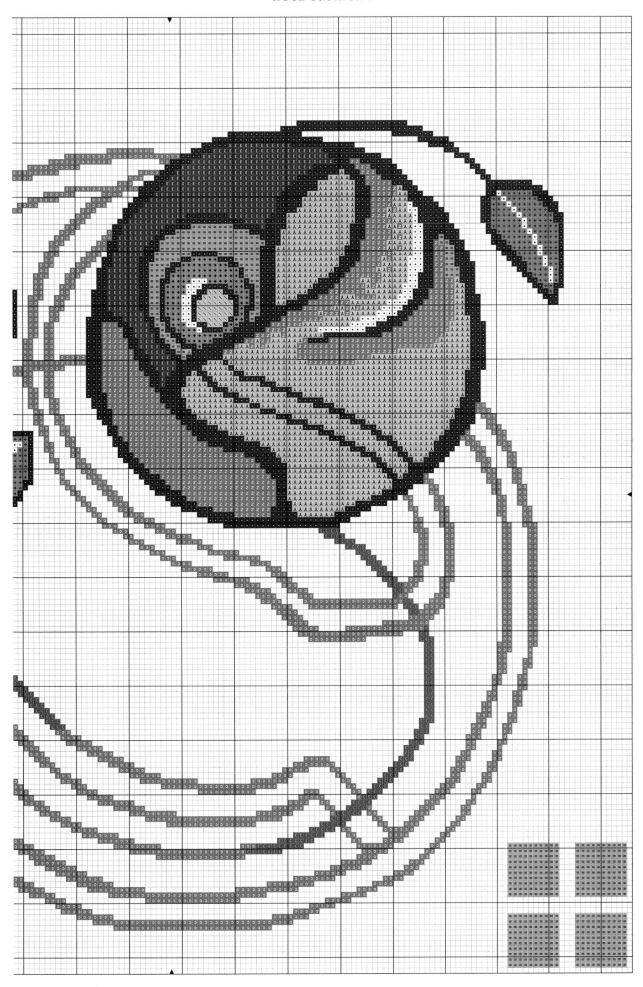

·Rose·Cushions·

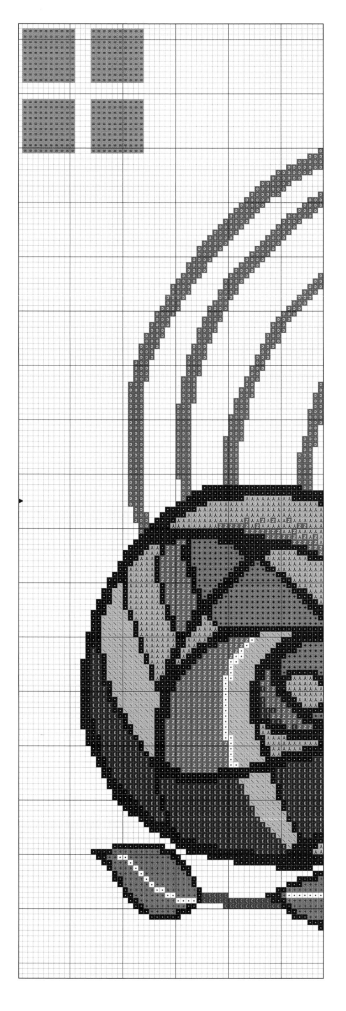

These lovely cushions were inspired by the distinctive Mackintosh rose and based on his drawings of 1901. They show how a simple motif can be developed into supremely stylish designs. They have been worked on Lincoln cloth, a cotton and linen fabric which has the appearance of evenweave and the convenience of an Aida because the weave is interlocked. It was chosen for these cushions because the designs leave much of the fabric exposed. For a more economical choice, use Aida.

DESIGN SIZE
12⅛ x 12⅛in (31.5 x 31.5cm) for a 16 x 16in
(40 x 40cm) cover
Stitch count: 174 x 174

•

MATERIALS (for one cushion)
• 20 x 20in (51 x 51cm) 14-count Zweigart Lincoln cloth
in cream (code E3327/99)
• Stranded cottons as listed in the key on page 84
• Size 24 tapestry needle
• Backing fabric in cream, pink or grey
• 2yd (2m) of piping cord
• Cushion pad 16in (40cm)

1   Neaten the edges of the fabric to prevent fraying using a machine zigzag stitch or hand stitching and then mark the central horizontal and vertical guidelines on the fabric with tacking (see page 120).

2   Follow the charts on pages 84 to 87 and working with two strands of stranded cotton over one group of threads, begin by outlining the rose.

3   Stitching the swirling grey lines is quite a challenge. If you find yourself getting lost I suggest adding extra guidelines in tacking every twenty threads.

4   When the embroidery is complete, remove the tacking guidelines, press and make up into a cushion (see page 124).

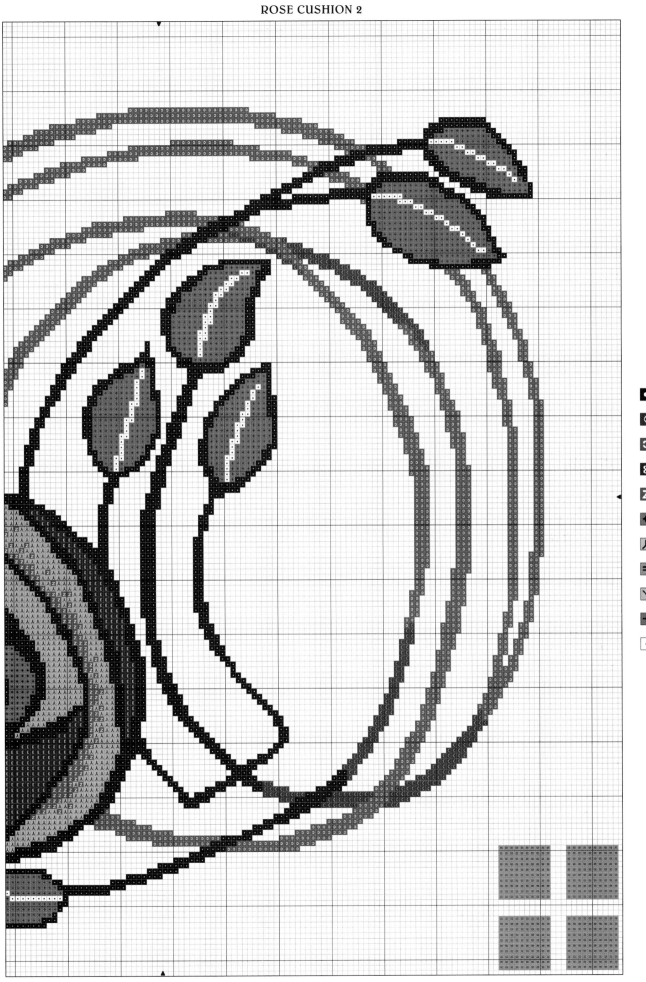

DMC

◨	413
◪	414
◖	318
Ɛ	3803
Z	3687
◆	3688
⅄	3689
=	554
◪	211
✦	3817
⋅	B5200

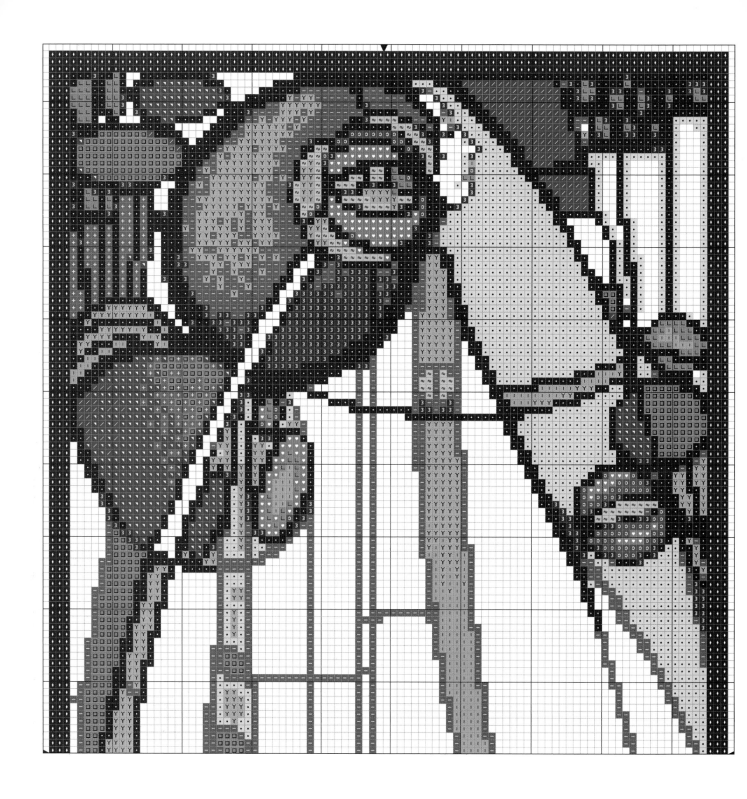

ROSE LADY PICTURE

DMC

♥	961	◣	798	Y	453
ↄ	3350	+	826	−	451
~	3689	◼	813	◉	844
◆	902	I	950	L	3778
╱	333	·	739	З	632

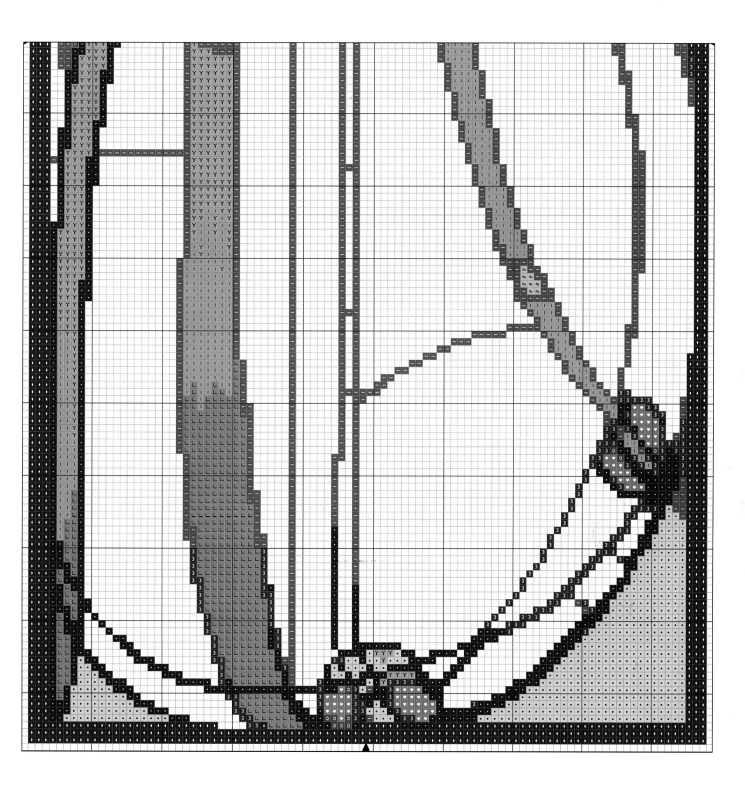

ROSE LADY PICTURE KEY

Colour	DMC	Anchor	Madeira	Skeins	Colour	DMC	Anchor	Madeira	Skeins
Dusty rose pink	961	76	0506	1	Peachy pink	950	376	2309	1
Dark rose	3350	69	0603	1	Antique ivory	739	1009	2014	1
Pale sugar pink	3689	49	0607	1	Light shell grey	453	231	1806	1
Dark garnet red	902	897	0601	1	Mid shell grey	451	233	1808	1
Dark violet	333	119	0903	1	Dark beaver grey	844	1041	1810	2
Dark blue	798	137	0912	1	Terracotta	3778	337	2310	1
Mid blue	826	136	1011	1	Brown	632	936	2311	1
Light blue	813	130	0909	1					

·Rose·Lady·Picture·

The design for this elegant lady came from an original Mackintosh stained glass panel. It is a three-quarter back view with her face looking out towards the right. The main focus of the picture (shown on page 83) is the rose decorating her hair at the top of the panel. Her long, pale robe takes on a raindrop shape, which can also be seen as a leaf or a bud, while the long peachy-pink curve suggests her right arm.

DESIGN SIZE
7 x 14in (17.5 x 35cm)
Stitch count: 97 x 194

•

MATERIALS
• 11 x 18in (30 x 46cm) 14-count Zweigart Aida in ivory
(code 264)
• Stranded cottons as listed in the key
• Size 24 tapestry needle

❧

1   Mark the central horizontal and vertical guidelines on the fabric with tacking (see page 120).

2   Following the charts on pages 88 and 89, work the design with two strands of stranded cotton and cross stitch throughout. It is best to begin at the series of vertical lines in mid shell grey and work all the outlines first, noticing that the lines change to dark beaver grey in places.

3   Cross stitch the coloured areas (which were coloured glass in the original Mackintosh design) and finally embroider the dark garnet red border to complete the picture.

4   Remove the tacking guidelines, press and frame (see page 123), leaving a margin of fabric showing round the border.

·Rose·Clock·

Enthused by the wide variety of clocks Mackintosh produced, I chose his design for a rose border to make this mantle clock. The flowing silver lines which originate at the hearts of the roses flow clockwise round the design, echoing the movement of the clock hands. The design has maximum impact on a black background, but it is not easy to sew, so use a good craft light and a magnifier.

❧

DESIGN SIZE
7½ x 7½in (19 x 19cm)
Stitch count: 135 x 135

•

MATERIALS
• 12 x 12in (30 x 30cm) 18-count Aida in black
• Stranded cottons as listed in the key
• Metallic threads as listed in the key
• Size 26 tapestry needle
• Mackintosh clock kit as shown, with exclusive case in hand-crafted, grey-stained ash and silver hands from Glyn Owen (see Suppliers page 126), *or* a separate clock movement and 40mm hands (sprayed silver) with your choice of surround

1   Mark the central horizontal and vertical guidelines on the fabric with tacking (see page 120). As it is important to count accurately when working this design to ensure the border joins up, you may find it best to add some extra guidelines.

2   Follow the charts on pages 92 and 93 and work with two strands of stranded cotton. The green is worked with two strands of stranded cotton plus one of blending filament (DMC Fil métallisé). The silver is used as it comes. Begin with the centre, followed by the white inner border.

3   To work the metallic leaf sections, begin each leaf by working the cross stitch, then the back stitch, taking stitches over two blocks at a time.

SINGING COLOUR AND METALLIC HIGHLIGHTS decorate this little mantle clock. The combination of curving roses and regular trellis demonstrate the tension between organic and geometric which fascinated Mackintosh. If you do not want to make a clock, you could just stitch the border for a photograph frame.

4 Embroider the roses, working the silver cross stitch lines last.

5 Check carefully that all embroidery is complete before removing the guidelines and pressing the embroidery, using a cloth between the iron and the metallic threads (see page 121).

6 Stretch the embroidered fabric over an 8¼ x 8¼in (21 x 21cm) board (see page 123). If you purchase the Glyn Owen kit the board is supplied, ready-cut and marked and with the mechanism attached. The kit comes with silver hands and a small central bevel. Assemble according to the manufacturer's instructions. If, however, you have used a clock movement with 40mm hands, make a small hole with a compass point in the exact centre. Fit the mechanism and select your choice of frame.

ROSE CLOCK KEY

Colour	DMC	Anchor	Madeira	Skeins
Leaf green	992	186	1202	1
Dark grey	413	236	1713	1
Mid grey	414	235	1801	1
White	B5200	1	white	1
Salmon pink	3708	26	0408	1
Light salmon	761	1021	0502	1
Bright pink	603	62	0701	1
Hot pink	893	40	0413	1
Red	3705	35	0410	1
Crimson	309	39	0507	1
Lavender	210	108	0802	1

Metallic threads

Silver	DMC Fil métallisé Art. 283 (or Kreinik Very Fine Braid (#4) col 001)
Green metallic	DMC Fil métallisé 4065 (or Kreinik Blending Filament 029)

ROSE CLOCK

DMC

H	992 + 4065 metallic		3708		3705
●	413	:	761	◥	309
‖	414	**n**	603	**L**	210
☐	B5200	/	893	**S**	Silver Art. 283

Back Stitch in:
———— 992 + 4065 metallic

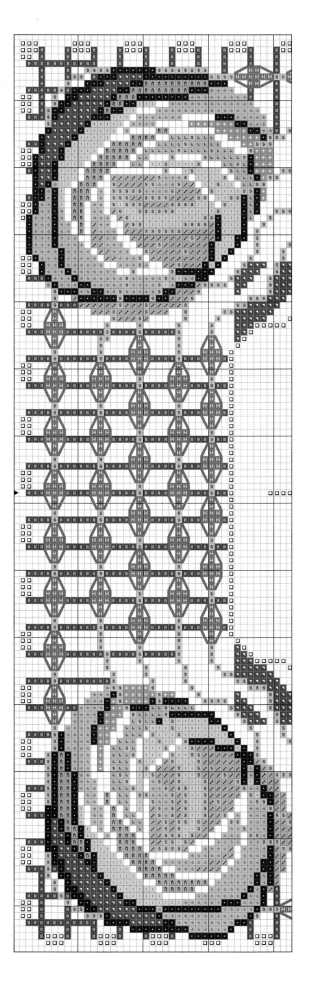

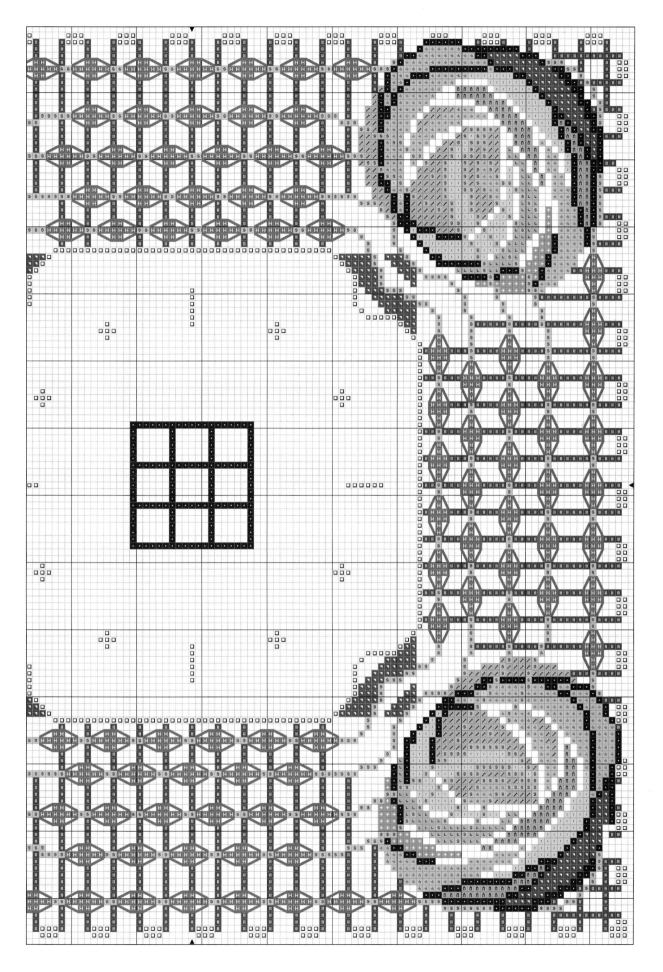

·Art·is·the·
·Flower·Picture·

he Mackintosh quotation featured in this picture (see photograph on page 2), 'Art is the flower, life is the green leaf', uses the typography he favoured. The typically elongated and simplified figure was inspired by the decoration from inside the left door of a writing cabinet he designed. I like the idea of decorating the inside instead of the outside; perhaps we should follow his example with our work-boxes.

❦

DESIGN SIZE
8 x 8in (20.5 x 20.5cm)
Stitch count: 135 x 137

•

MATERIALS

• 12 x 12in (30 x 30cm) 18-count Zweigart Aida in platinum (code 770)
• Stranded cottons as listed in the key
• Size 26 tapestry needle

❦

1 Mark the central horizontal and vertical guidelines on the fabric with tacking (see page 120).

2 Following the chart and counting out from the central guidelines, start stitching the quotation using two strands of stranded cotton for the cross stitch. Work all the cross stitch before starting the back stitch.

3 When working the back stitch, the lettering and green leaf use two strands. Use one strand for the figure and flower. There are a few three-quarter cross stitches around the mouth, neck and hair (see page 122 for how to work these).

ART IS THE FLOWER KEY

Colour	DMC	Anchor	Madeira	Skeins
Dark green	986	246	1313	1
White	blanc	1	white	1
Black	310	403	black	1
Silver grey	3023	392	1902	1
Dark rose	3350	69	0603	1
Mid rose	961	76	0506	1
Light rose	3716	25	0606	1
Salmon pink	894	26	0414	1
Dark violet	333	119	0903	1
Light tan	3827	363	2301	1

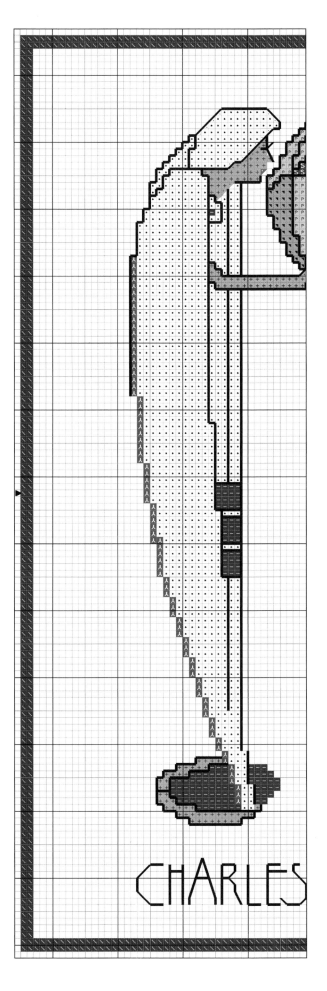

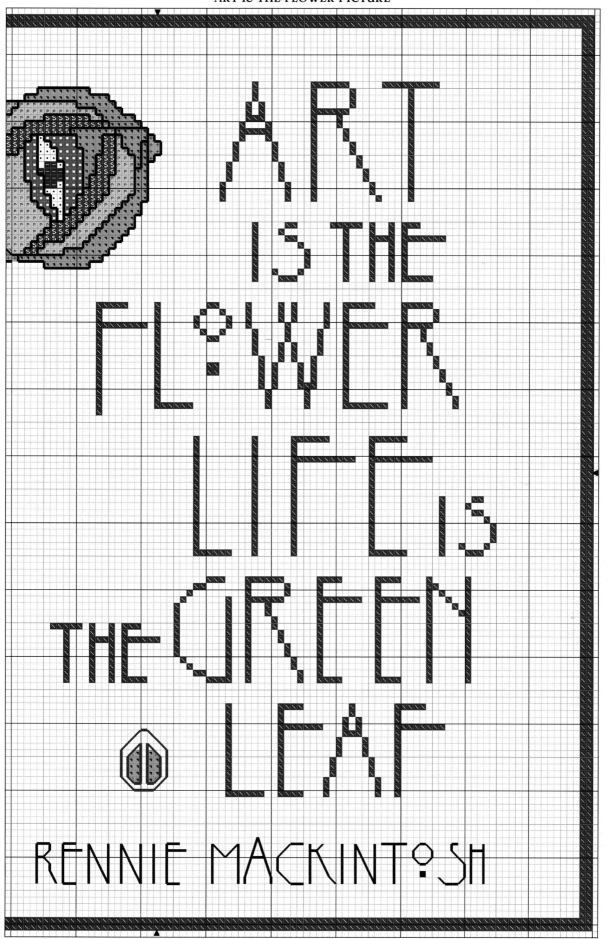

DMC

◤	986
·	Blanc
■	310
⅄	3023
S	3350
▢	961
P	3716
◣	894
▬	333
✚	3827

Back Stitch in:
——— 986
——— 310

·THE·WHITE·ROSE·AND·THE·RED·ROSE·

THIS CHAPTER FEATURES the work of Margaret Macdonald Mackintosh who was one of a talented group of women working as professional artists in Glasgow at the turn of the century. She had studied at the Glasgow School of Art with her sister Frances and had then set up a studio where they painted and produced decorative metalwork, embroidery and jewellery. Other notable women in their circle were Jessie Newbery and Jessie King, who designed a popular range of silver jewellery for Liberty.

In 1900 Margaret married Charles Rennie Mackintosh and they worked in close collaboration. Margaret designed and made decorative panels which were inset in the furniture; she embroidered banners and created large decorative panels for interior decorating projects, including the Willow Tea Rooms. Sometimes she and Charles shared the designing of panels for one space, so of course the style was very similar but it was an equal partnership. In fact he said, 'Margaret has genius,

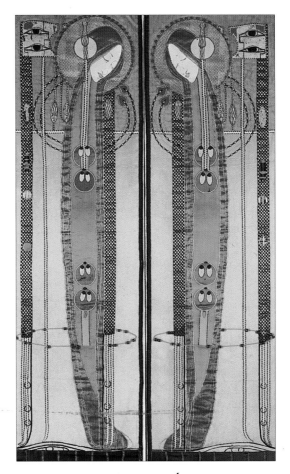

MARGARET'S APPLIQUÉ PANEL with embroidery and beads from 1900 is as much an abstract arrangement of colour and line as a picture of two women.

I have only talent'.

The inspiration for The White Rose and The Red Rose design is a panel for the Rose Boudoir for the 1902 Turin Exhibition. It faced a second panel called 'The Heart of the Rose' which also shows the two women, with one holding a baby which lies at the centre of a large, dark red rose. As both Margaret and Frances were Symbolist artists, it seems a fair interpretation to suggest that the white rose represents youth and innocence, whilst the other represents maturity, fertility and experience. Both figures are closely bound together by a network of curving lines and both are integrated with nature in the form of the rose boughs that circle round them. Both panels were painted in golds, pinks and green in a style that contrasts areas of detail and lots of linear decoration with large, empty areas of gold. In the picture and pot lids, I have cross stitched over loosely woven, sheer metallic gauze fabric to mimic Margaret's use of appliqué on her embroidered panels. ❦ ❦

THE WHITE ROSE AND THE RED ROSE PICTURE combines the swooping curves so typical of Art Nouveau with an innovative use of applied gauze to add a shimmering texture to cross stitch embroidery.

·The·White·Rose·and· ·The·Red·Rose·Picture·

Margaret Macdonald Mackintosh used appliqué in her embroidered banners and I have adapted the idea to this design, using a loosely woven, sheer metallic gold gauze fabric through which it is possible to see the holes of the Aida. It is an interesting technique that adds a new dimension to cross stitch work though I would recommend it for an embroiderer with patience and experience. The sheer gauze is tacked down and cross stitch worked over it. When the edges of the dress have been worked the sheer gauze is cut away.

DESIGN SIZE
12 x 14in (30 x 35cm)
Stitch count: 192 x 222

•

MATERIALS
• 18 x 18in (46 x 46cm) 18-count Zweigart Aida
in ecru (code 13)
• 12 x 12in (30 x 30cm) of loosely woven sheer gold
gauze fabric (allowing the needle to pass through
easily – see Suppliers page 126)
• Stranded cottons as listed in the key
• Size 26 tapestry needle and a crewel needle

❦

1   If the sheer gauze fabric you have chosen frays very badly, first seal the very edges with a little fabric glue. Attach the sheer gauze to the Aida by first marking the centre of both pieces with pins. Place the centre of the sheer gauze over the centre of the Aida, making sure that the grain of the weave is square with the Aida. Pin in the centre and round the edges, then place face down on a flat surface and, beginning in the middle, tack in place (see Fig 1). If you have done any quilting you may be familiar with this grid-like tacking procedure. Mark the centre horizontal and vertical lines and then the diagonals. If you use a different coloured tacking thread and count every twenty lines then you will provide a grid for reference that will be helpful during the embroidery.

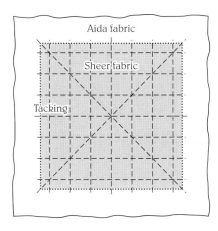

Fig 1 Tacking the Aida and sheer fabric together.

2   Mount the joined fabrics in an embroidery frame and following the charts on pages 100–103 begin stitching near the centre with two strands of stranded cotton. Where cross stitch is worked through the sheer gauze it may be easier to use a crewel needle. I also recommend a magnifier and a strong light. When working the large pink areas, work the two rows of outlining stitches and then cut away the area to be filled in with cross stitch.

3   When the cross stitch on the dress areas is complete, use embroidery scissors to trim back the gauze but do not try to cut around every stitch – follow the curve smoothly and do not worry about a small gold margin (see Fig 2).

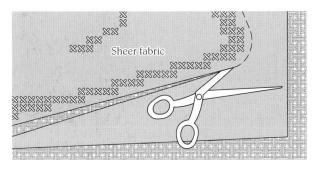

Fig 2 Trimming the sheer fabric.

4   Once the dress has been trimmed round close to the stitching, embroider the heads, the long lines and rose decorations in the corners.

5   When the embroidery is complete, remove the guidelines, and press gently at a low temperature with a dry iron. Use a pressing cloth between the embroidery and the iron (see page 121). I would not recommend washing this piece.

·Trinket·Pot·Lids·

The use of sheer fabric under cross stitching has been used again on a smaller scale for two trinket pot lids, based on the corner decoration in The White Rose and The Red Rose Picture.

DESIGN SIZES
Large lid 3in (7.5cm); Medium lid 2in (5cm)
Stitch counts: Large lid 37 x 33; Medium lid 25 x 23

•

MATERIALS
FOR THE LARGE LID DESIGN
• 7 x 7in (18 x 18cm) 14-count Aida in ecru (colour 13)
3 x 3in (7.5 x 7.5cm) scrap of pink metallic gauze
(loosely woven so the needle can pass easily – see
Suppliers page 126)
• Stranded cottons as listed in the key
• 5 x 5in (13 x 13cm) iron-on interfacing
• Large brass trinket pot (see Suppliers page 126)
FOR THE MEDIUM LID DESIGN
• 6 x 6in (15 x 15cm) 14-count Aida in ecru (colour 13)
2 x 2in (5 x 5cm) scrap of pink metallic gauze, as above
• Stranded cottons as listed in the key
• Iron-on interfacing 5 x 5in (13 x 13cm)
• Medium brass trinket pot (see Suppliers page 126)

1   To stitch either design, first pin the square of gauze centrally onto the Aida, tacking round the edges to hold it in place.

2   Following the relevant pot lid chart and using a size 24 tapestry needle, begin stitching the rose outline near the top of the gauze using two strands of stranded cotton for the cross stitch and the back stitch.

3   Once all the roses have been stitched, carefully cut the gauze away from them (see step 3, page 98), then embroider the leaves and stems.

4   Iron on the interfacing using a dry iron and a very moderate heat, just hot enough to fuse the interfacing. Cut out the designs and mount them in the pot lids, following the manufacturer's instructions.

POT LIDS KEY

Colour	DMC	Anchor	Madeira
Dark mauve pink	315	1019	0810
Rose red	3350	69	0603
Light green	563	204	1207
Dark grey	317	400	1714

MEDIUM POT LID

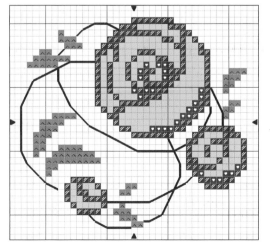

POT LIDS

DMC

▨ 315

♥ 3350

◤ 563

▢ Applied pink fabric

Back Stitch in:
————317

LARGE POT LID

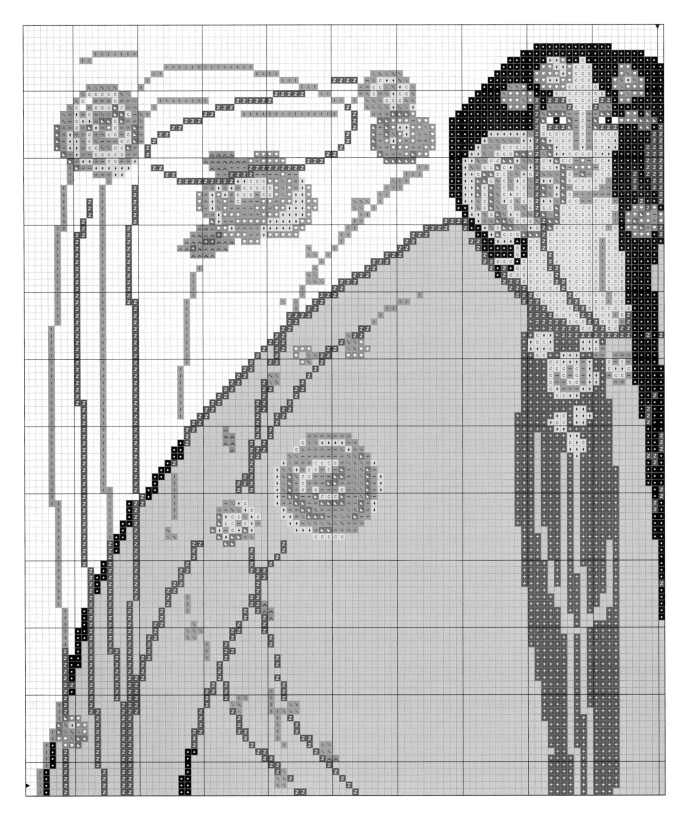

THE WHITE ROSE AND THE RED ROSE PICTURE KEY

Colour	DMC	Anchor	Madeira	Skeins	Colour	DMC	Anchor	Madeira	Skeins
Black	310	403	black	2	Light plum	3688	1016	0605	1
Mid grey	317	400	1714	2	Pale pink	818	271	0608	1
Silver grey	318	399	1802	1	Leaf green	3814	189	1203	1
Mauve pink	3726	1018	0810	1	Light green	563	204	1207	1
Light mauve pink	3727	1016	0809	2	Creamy flesh	3770	1009	0306	1
Rose red	3350	69	0603	1					

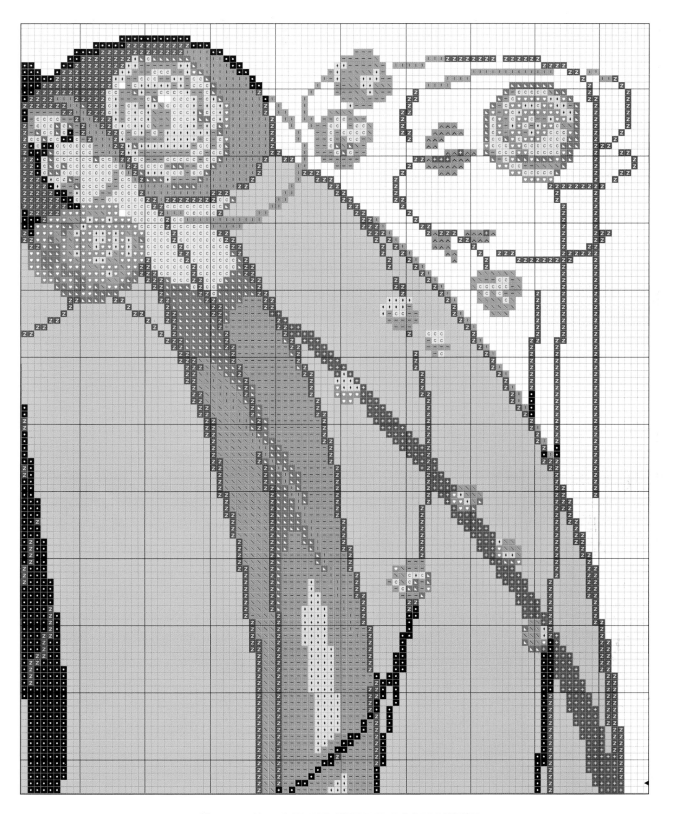

THE WHITE ROSE AND THE RED ROSE PICTURE

DMC

■	310	—	3727	+	3814	
Z	317	♥	3350	∧	563	
I	318	◥	3688	C	3770	
◣	3726	◆	818		Applied gold fabric	

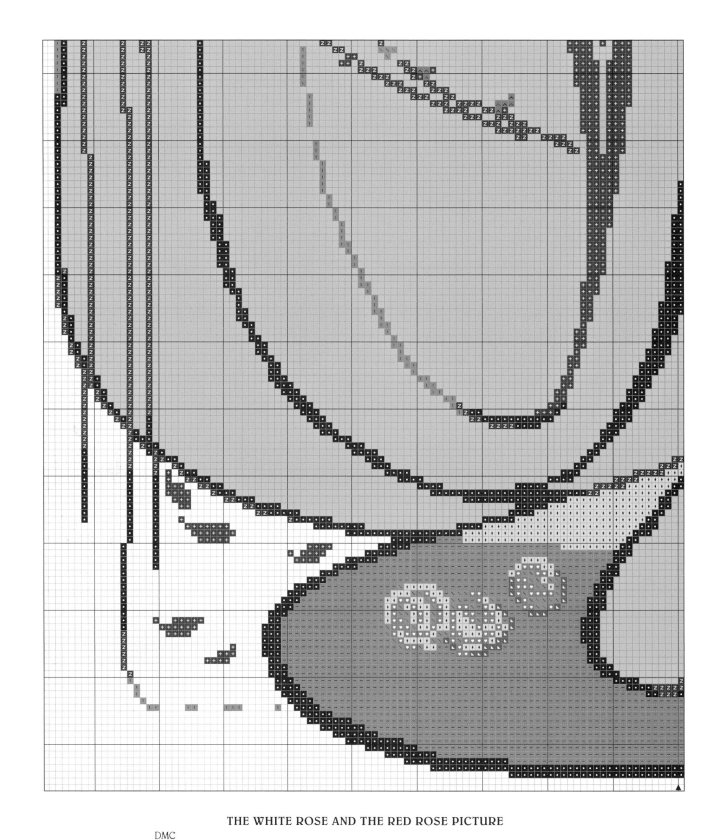

THE WHITE ROSE AND THE RED ROSE PICTURE

DMC

■ 310	▮ 318	▬ 3727	◣ 3688	✚ 3814	C 3770
Z 317	◤ 3726	♥ 3350	♦ 818	◢ 563	▢ Applied gold fabric

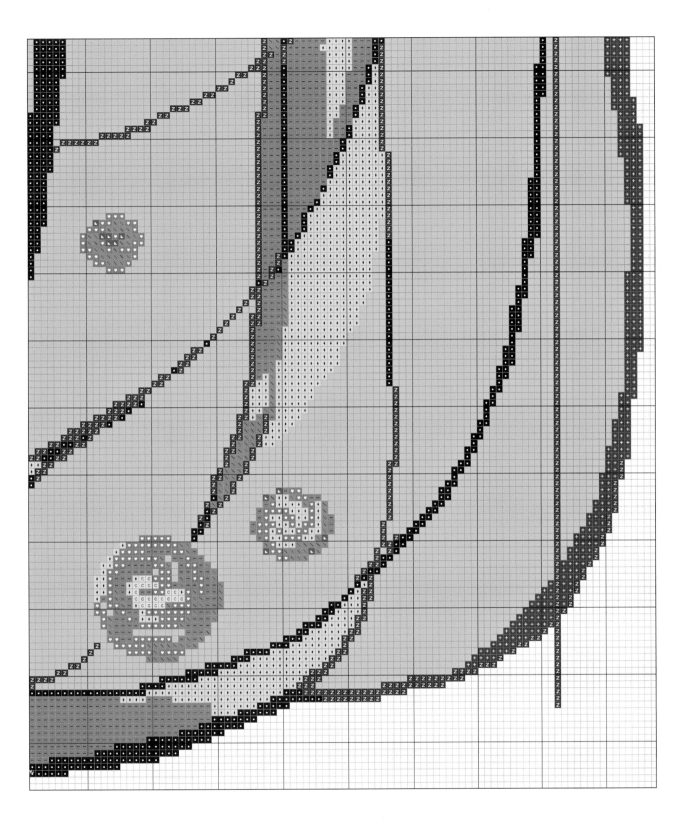

·SMALL·MOTIFS·FOR·DESIGN·IDEAS·

THE PAGES WHICH FOLLOW are packed with ideas for small projects. They are a starting point for your own ideas; charted in colour but with the choice of yarn colour and fabric left to you. A selection of designs has been made up (shown opposite).

The lily picture is based on a design in René Beauclair's book *Dessins d'Ornamentation*. All his designs feature abstract plant shapes in elegant patterns with a hint of Celtic interlace design. The lily (charted page 107) was worked on white 18-count Aida to fit a 4 x 6in (10 x 15cm) frame.

The napkin corner rose design is adapted from an embroidery by the Glasgow artist Jessie Newbery. Repeated in four corners it would make a pretty cushion cover. This piece was stitched on 28-count Quaker Cloth, worked over two threads (see chart page 111).

The flying crane designs in blue and white are perfect for decorating many items, such as coasters, pot lids and book covers (see charts page 108/109). The birds were adapted from a tile design by William de Morgan and were stitched on 18-count Aida using two shades of blue stranded cotton.

The pair of peacocks (charted but not illustrated) evolved from a fabric design. They are charted on page 108 in a single colour but you could include other colours to the tail, or add beads or sequins, or work parts in metallic braids. The butterfly and dragonfly motifs (charted on page 106) are taken from jewellery designs and might also benefit from added beads or iridescent sequins. The peacock feather design (charted on page 109) was made with a note book cover in mind. The colouring shown works best on a very dark fabric.

The pincushion shown is a very simple lily of the valley design (charted on page 111). It is worked on a 14-count Aida with two strands of stranded cotton. Try working it on a needlecase with the design mirrored for the back.

The square tulip coaster shown opposite and charted on page 110 is one of three tulip designs based on Art Nouveau tiles. Worked on 18-count Aida they fit standard square coasters but would also make pretty cards. Worked on a larger scale, with a border design, they would be suitable for other items, such as oven gloves and tea cosies.

The square rose card (charted page 111) is worked on 14-count Aida and is one of several derived from the Glasgow school, where a simple heart motif often accompanied rose decorations. The hawthorn, orange flower and lily of the valley motifs (charted pages 106, 110 and 111) have been repeated to suggest the possibilities of building up more elaborate designs from simple motifs. ❧ ❧

A SELECTION OF DESIGNS made up into small items, showing the many creative possibilities of Art Nouveau motifs. They include a little lily picture, a rose napkin, flying crane book cover, pot and coaster, a lily of the valley pincushion, a tulip coaster and a rose card.

BUTTERFLY   DRAGONFLY

HAWTHORN
GROUPING

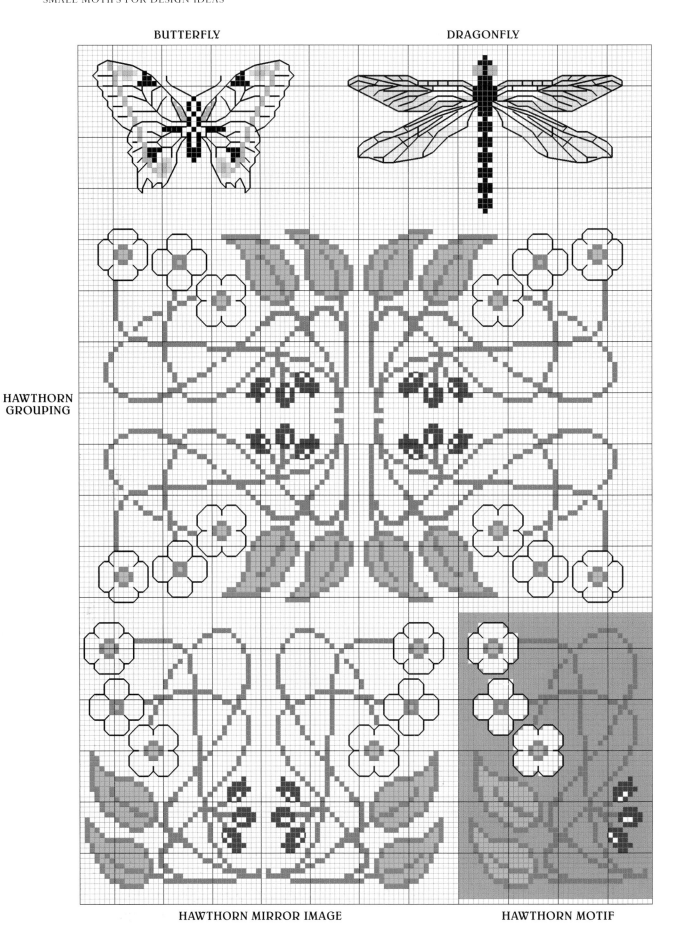

HAWTHORN MIRROR IMAGE   HAWTHORN MOTIF

PURPLE FLOWER SPRAY   INTERLACED SHIELD   TULIP BOOKMARK

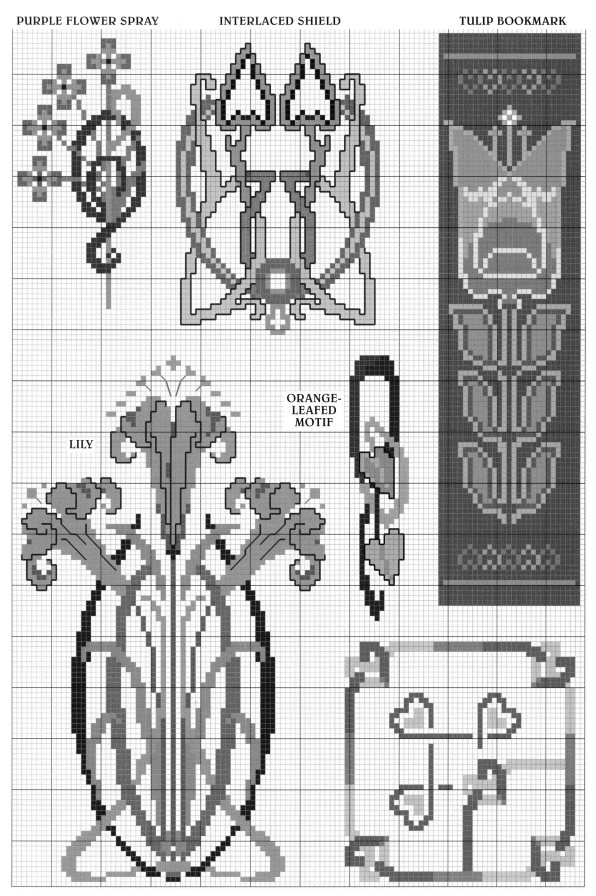

LILY

ORANGE-
LEAFED
MOTIF

INTERLACED HEART EDGINGS

PAIR OF PEACOCKS　　　　**FLYING CRANE COASTER**

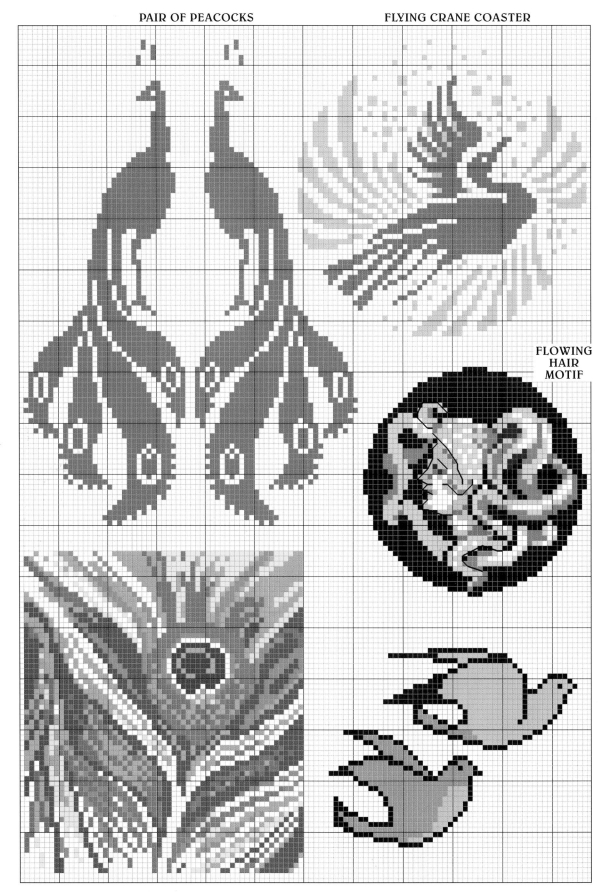

**FLOWING
HAIR
MOTIF**

PEACOCK FEATHER CLOSE UP　　　　**TWO BIRDS FLYING**

FLYING CRANE PEN POT   **PEACOCK FEATHER**

FLYING CRANE NOTEBOOK COVER   **CRANE**

THREE TULIPS IN A VASE **ORANGE FLOWER MOTIFS**

THREE TULIPS WITH LONG STEMS

MOTH

TWO TULIPS **SINGLE TULIP** **ELONGATED TULIP**

GLASGOW ROSE CARD   GLASGOW ROSE CORNER

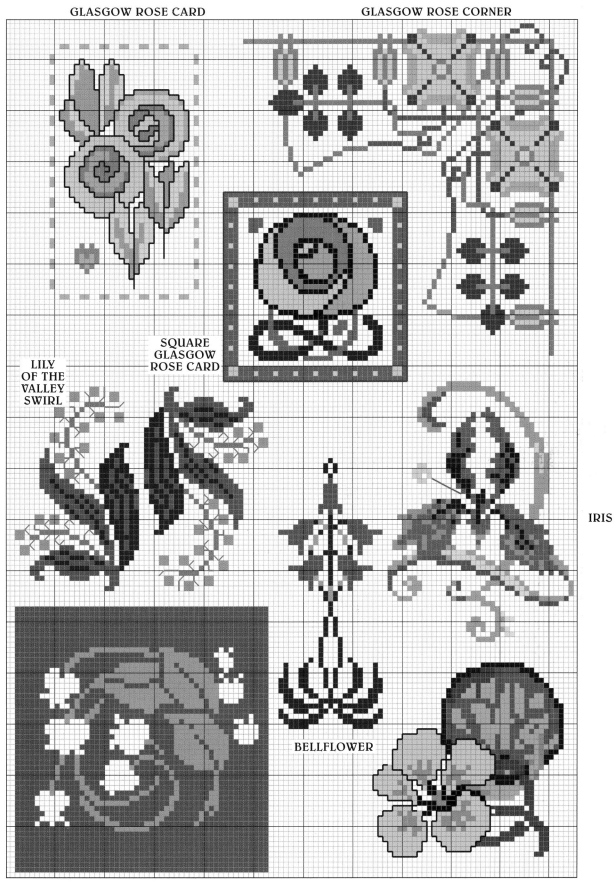

SQUARE
GLASGOW
ROSE CARD

LILY
OF THE
VALLEY
SWIRL

IRIS

BELLFLOWER

LILY OF THE VALLEY SPIRAL   NASTURTIUM

111

·DECORATIVE·BORDERS·

THE BORDER DESIGNS shown stitched here, and others charted on pages 113–118, are for you to use creatively. Many of them are adapted from design books of the period. The artists of that time changed colours arbitrarily to suit their decorative schemes and you can do the same.

Borders are useful, decorative and fun to work. Used alone they are suitable for guest towels, tray cloths, runners, bell pulls, children's clothes, aprons, even bibs. If repeated on four sides of a square, they produce an instant cushion design, or they can be used in strips like the two shown on the William de Morgan bolster cushion. Just one border placed centrally or one third from the edge of the fabric can be dramatic, particularly if you edge the border with one or more rows of ribbon.

If you want to turn a corner with a border the simplest way is to butt a horizontal length up against a vertical one; as in the border of the snowdrop cushion on page 79. It is worth considering which part of the design comes to a natural looking break. If the border is made up of distinct motifs then stopping in between is an obvious solution. Sometimes it is necessary to leave out an overlapping bit of the next motif. If the space to be filled makes this solution impractical just cover the

design with a piece of paper and move it up and down the border till you find a cut-off point which looks right.

An alternative way of joining borders at corners is to cut the border at 45 degrees, though this is not so good with borders that are asymmetrical. To chose the best place to make the mitred join, hold a small mirror over the border with the bottom edge at a 45 degree angle across the design. Move it along the border until you find a pleasing result.

If you want to apply an embroidered band to another fabric use ready finished Aida or linen band or a strip of Aida, which allows a greater choice of width and colour. Turn the edges under and stitch down by machine, or neaten the edges and cover the join with braid or ribbon in a toning colour. Where a border has a line of colour along the edge, you could fold the edge over and work through a double thickness to neaten, or substitute a buttonhole stitch row for the outside row of cross stitch.

Borders are easy to stitch and can create instant effects or give added emphasis to a single central motif. Even the simplest motif when repeated can produce a pleasing and rhythmic design. Why not look through some Art Nouveau sourcebooks and create your own? ❦ ❦

A SELECTION of Art Nouveau-inspired borders (charted pages 113–118), to give ideas for creative possibilities.

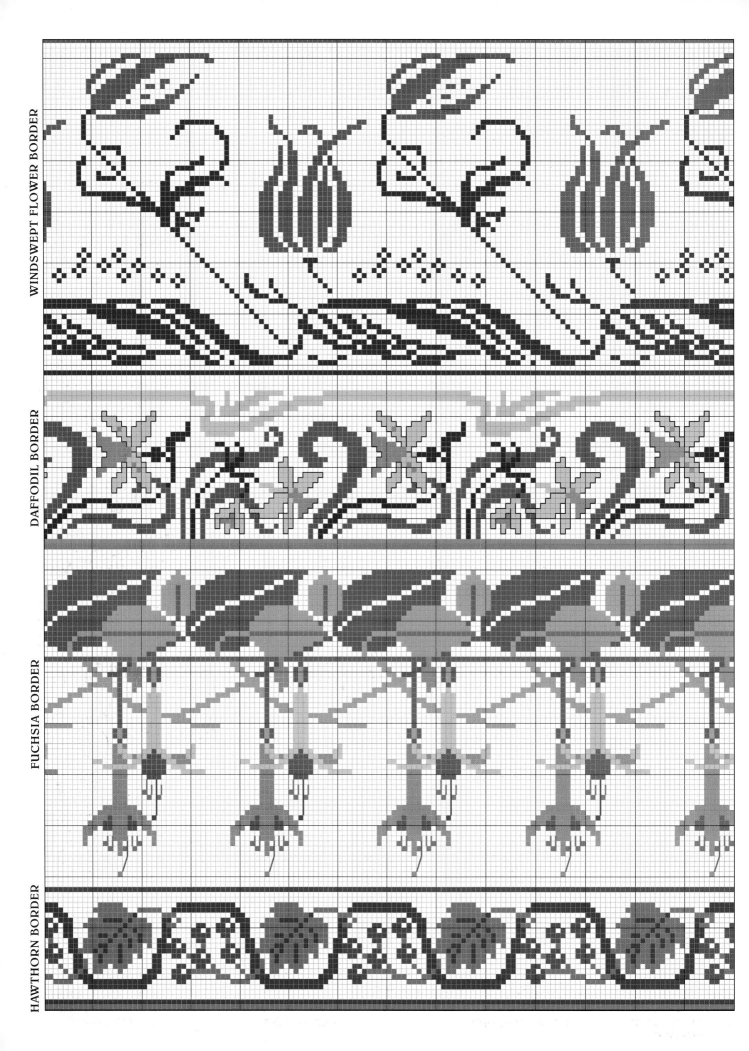

WINDSWEPT FLOWER BORDER

DAFFODIL BORDER

FUCHSIA BORDER

HAWTHORN BORDER

SOLOMAN'S SEAL BORDER   **WISTERIA BORDER**   **IRIS BORDER**   **TEASEL BORDER**

LILY OF THE VALLEY BORDER

SNOWDROP BORDER

MUCHA POPPY BORDER

TULIP BORDER

INTERTWINED MUCHA
CARNATION BORDER

BLUE LEAVES BORDER

MUCHA ROSE BORDER

SNAIL BORDER

DE MORGAN LEAVES BORDER

GLASGOW REPEAT ROSE BORDER   GLASGOW TWO ROSE BORDER   TULIP BORDER   GREEN FLOWER BORDER

·BASIC·TECHNIQUES·

Those who have not done much embroidery before may find the following pages useful.

·Fabrics·

Each project gives the fabric required for working the piece as shown in the accompanying photograph, but you could substitute one fabric for another.

The blockweave fabrics, such as Aida, are probably the simplest to work. The weave locks each block of threads in place, resulting in a very stable, firm fabric.

'Evenweave' just means that there are the same number of warp threads as weft threads to the inch or centimetre. The higher the thread count number, the more threads or blocks of threads there are to the inch. Evenweave is usually embroidered over two threads at a time. Thus a 28-count (or 28 holes per inch) evenweave fabric can be substituted for a 14-count Aida, a 32-count evenweave for a 16-count Aida, and vice versa.

Calculating the Design Size

As you gain confidence you may choose to work on a larger or smaller count of fabric. This will, of course, result in the finished piece being a slightly different size. To find out how large a piece would become, divide the stitch count given by the number of holes per inch of the fabric. For example, the iris border on page 115 is 48 stitches wide. To find out how wide it would be if worked on a 14-count fabric, simply divide 48 by 14. The result is almost $3\frac{1}{2}$in (8.5cm).

Remember that most designs need a margin of blank fabric around the edge of the stitched area, plus an extra 2in (5cm) on all sides to allow for any framing. The fabric amount stated in the projects allows for this. Where measurements are given, the width is usually quoted first, followed by the height.

·Threads·

Many of the projects described use stranded cottons, with which most people are familiar. I used DMC stranded cottons but if you prefer one of the alternatives given, bear in mind that they are not always an exact colour match. The names of the colours I have used are for convenience and are not official colour names which manufacturers will recognise. Always order by the code number. Divide skeins into lengths of about 20in (50cm) and divide each length into its six strands, then recombine the number needed – usually two.

Metallic braid is used as it comes. Blending filament is used in conjunction with stranded cottons. I thread a length along with the cotton, but the packs show other ways of knotting the thread to the needle, which you may wish to try. Tapestry wool is available in skeins and some colours come in hanks. I have not given alternatives for the colours in the Peacock Rug because I could not match the colours well enough from other manufacturer's ranges. Anchor Tappiserie wool is quite easy to find, but if you have problems contact the telephone numbers in the Suppliers list on page 126.

·Needles·

All the embroidery is done with blunt-ended tapestry needles, except for parts of The White Rose and The Red Rose Picture, where you can use a crewel needle. Beading needles are required to attach seed beads. I have recommended needle sizes, but you may prefer a different size – it is a matter of compromise between having a large enough eye to take the thread and a size of needle which will pass through the fabric holes without too much friction.

·General·Accessories·

Apart from fabric, thread and needles you must have a good pair of embroidery scissors with sharp points, as well as cutting-out scissors. I also think a bright light is essential. Many are made especially for embroidery, but a studio-type light will do just as well. It is important to position it correctly. When working on dark fabrics it is really helpful to place a brightly reflective sheet of paper or white pillowslip over your knees. This will make the holes in the fabric show up much more clearly. You may find working some of the designs in this book much easier with a magnifier.

·Embroidery·Frames·

I recommend using a frame for any evenweave fabric and when working with a mixture of threads, as you may find that their different characteristics cause you to pull some threads more firmly than others. Where there are layers of fabric, as in The White Rose and The Red Rose Picture, a frame is necessary. Small pieces of fabric and rug canvas can be worked without a frame and it is certainly much easier to roll up the fabric and take it about with you if it is not framed.

For small pieces use a hoop frame (Fig 1) or flexi hoop (Fig 2). Always try to use a hoop large enough to take the whole design. If this is not possible, only leave the hoop on the work whilst you are actually embroidering, and take care when repositioning it not to let the edge coincide with an embroidered area.

Fig 1 Hoop frame.   *Fig 2 Flexi hoop.*

For larger pieces, a rectangular 'slate' frame (Fig 3) is the traditional answer. The embroidery fabric is stitched to a tape attached to the top and bottom rails, matching the centre of the tape to the centre of the embroidery

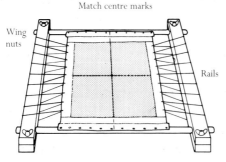

Match centre marks

Wing
nuts

Rails

Fig 3 Rectangular slate frame.

fabric. The frame has wing nuts which can be loosened to allow the rails to be rotated to roll the fabric up if it is larger than the frame, for example a bell pull. The edges of the selected area are laced to the sides of the frame to keep the fabric taut. This type of frame gives good, firm support, and is particularly suitable if the embroidery is to be left where it is.

A rectangular clip frame is made from lengths of plastic tube (Fig 4). These come with different lengths of tube which are assembled with plastic corner pieces. The fabric is placed over the tubes and clipped in place, using extra tubes, slit along their length. This light and convenient frame is particularly suitable for use where part of a large amount of fabric is being worked.

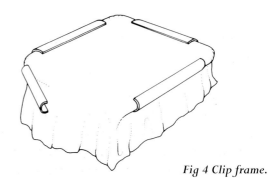

Fig 4 Clip frame.

·To·Begin·

Although it is tempting simply to thread your needle and begin to stitch, you may find that you soon encounter difficulties. These can be easily avoided by following the simple advice given below.

Preparing the Fabric

When working on Aida I find that cutting it out with pinking shears stops it from fraying. When using evenweave, I like to neaten the edge by using a machine zigzag stitch or by overcasting the edges by hand.

Centre lines are indicated on the charts by the use of opposing arrows. Find the centre of your fabric by folding it in half both ways. Mark the centre lines in sewing thread, using a tacking stitch. Make sure, especially when using evenweave, that the line of stitches stays straight along the grain of the fabric. In some of the larger designs I have suggested marking extra guide lines and it is wise to choose another colour for these.

Following the Charts

Each coloured square on the charts represents one cross stitch. The keys accompanying the charts list the threads used, their colours and codes (including alternatives to DMC stranded cottons where appropriate). In some cases I have used similar shades in the embroidery and so symbols have been added to aid identification in all projects except the Borders and Small Motifs. A few of the designs use quarter or three-quarter cross stitches; these are represented by a square divided diagonally, with the relevant section coloured and containing the symbol. Where back stitch is used it is represented by a thick coloured line with the colour given in the key. The charts show slightly more pronounced grid lines after every ten squares to help you count.

You may want to use the charts straight from the book or you can photocopy them in colour for your own use. This allows you to enlarge or reduce and tape various sections of the larger charts together. It also allows you to cross off areas as you work them, which some people find helpful. You can also draw in the centre lines and any extra guidelines in felt pen to match the lines you have worked. Generally I start embroidering at the centre and work blocks of colour at a time.

Although this book is devoted to cross stitch, the charts could also be used for canvaswork (needlepoint) embroidery. Simply use half cross stitch or petit point (tent stitch) instead of cross stitch. Remember you will need to add a background colour to most of the designs, though not the Peacock Rug which could be worked on a finer canvas. Designs which rely on back stitch detail are not really suitable for canvaswork.

Starting to Stitch

To begin stitching in an empty area of fabric, first knot the thread and take it through the fabric from the front about 1in (2.5cm) from where you wish to begin. When you have stitched over the thread the knot can be safely trimmed off and the end persuaded through to the back. To start a new thread in a stitched area, just thread it under four or five stitches on the back of the work before beginning to stitch. These techniques eliminate ugly bumps that could spoil the look of the finished piece.

·To·Finish·

To finish off an area of stitching, thread your needle back through the last four or five stitches on the wrong side of the fabric and then trim the thread.

Pressing

A finished piece of embroidery will need careful pressing to smooth out the fabric and correct any distortion without flattening the stitches and spoiling the texture. A layer of towel covered with a piece of sheet should give a soft enough surface to rest the embroidery. Lay the embroidery face down, pull it into shape making sure the grain of the fabric is straight. Press it gently on the back at a heat suitable for the type of fabric and thread. Do not use steam on metallic threads and cover the piece with a pressing cloth. Cottons embroidered on Aida or cotton cloth can be pressed at the two- or three-spot setting on the iron; any piece using synthetics, wool or silk, require the one-spot setting.

Cleaning

Wash embroidery in water as hot as the fabric will stand using a mild detergent, thoroughly dissolved in water. If the colour bleeds, separate the item from other pieces of embroidery, wash it thoroughly but without rubbing, and rinse until all trace of the stain disappears. Never leave the embroidery wet. Remove excess water by rolling the item in a towel and squeezing it gently. Dry it flat then iron from the back whilst still damp.

Stretching

To stretch an embroidered canvas you will need a clean board larger than the canvas, rust-proof tacks or small nails and a set square. Begin by nailing the canvas right side down onto the board, starting in the centre of one side. You could dampen the canvas. Add nails at intervals all along the side to one corner and then the other, making sure the canvas is fixed straight against the line. Now begin tacking the canvas down onto the board on the other side, measuring and stretching to ensure it is square. Finish the other sides in the same way. Once you are satisfied that the measurements and angles are correct add more nails all around until the edges are straight. Leave in a warm place for about two days, then pull out the nails and finish your rug or piece.

·Stitches·

Cross Stitch

Cross stitch is the basic stitch used in this book (Figs 5 and 6). Either make individual crosses, or work half crosses along a line then return, stitching over the half crosses in the opposite direction. The first method is the most stable and unlikely to cause fabric distortion, and is to be preferred if working without a frame. However, as long as you develop an even tension without pulling the stitch so tightly that it distorts the fabric threads, either is acceptable. It is important to choose which direction your top stitch will go and stick to it, otherwise the texture will be uneven.

Fig 5 Cross stitch on Aida.   *Fig 6 Cross stitch on evenweave.*

Three-Quarter Cross Stitch

Work a quarter stitch from the corner into the centre, then work a half stitch in the normal way (Fig 7). The rule of having the top stitches always lying in the same direction is thus sometimes broken.

Fig 7 Three-quarter cross stitch.

Back Stitch

This is an easy outline stitch that is used in a few projects in this book. Look at the chart and instructions to see if it should be worked with one or two strands of stranded cotton. It is usually worked after the cross stitching. Bring the needle through the fabric from the back and take a stitch backwards. Bring the needle up again at the far end of the next stitch along the line and then take another stitch backwards to fill in the gap (Fig 8). Work over the same unit of fabric – one block or two threads – as you have used for the cross stitch.

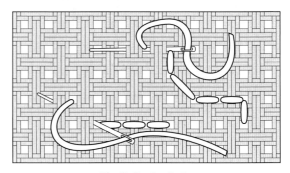

Fig 8 Back stitch.

Double Running Stitch

This is suitable for long lines. Make a line of running stitches then turn back and fill in all the gaps with another row of running stitches (see Fig 9). For the smoothest line, when working the return line of running stitches, put your needle through the fabric to the left of the first row thread and bring it up to the right of it, or vice versa (be consistent).

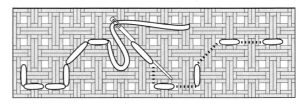

Fig 9 Double running stitch.

Petit Point or Tent Stitch

This stitch is a variation of half cross stitch, which is used when working over one thread of a non-interlocked fabric. In this book it has only been used for the purple and pink flower border on page 114, which is worked over one intersection of Hardanger fabric. Use it if you adapt any pattern to work over one thread of evenweave fabric. It is the same stitch that is used in canvaswork (needlepoint) on a non-interlocked canvas. It can be worked diagonally or in rows (Fig 10) and differs from half cross stitch in having a longer stitch on the back of the fabric than on the front. This is essential to maintain the stability of the design and fabric. It is recommended that this stitch is worked with the fabric on a frame.

Fig 10 Petit point (over one thread of evenweave).

Plaited Cross Stitch Edging

This is recommended for finishing off the Peacock Rug on page 27. Starting a little way from a corner, work from right to left along the folded edge of the canvas. Hold the wool along the top edge as shown in stage 1 of Fig 11. Bring the wool through from the back at A, then take the wool over the loose end and through from the back again at B. The wool is then taken back to A and brought through from the back again to form the first cross. The wool always passes from the back to the front of the canvas. For stage 2, take the wool forward three squares to C. Cross back to B then go forwards three holes. Continue, always counting three holes forwards, then two back, and always taking the wool through from the back to the front.

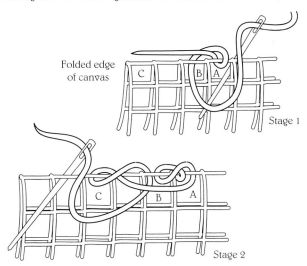

Fig 11 Plaited cross stitch edging.

·Making·Up·

Pictures

To make your work up into a picture you can simply press it and take it to a framer specialising in embroidery who will do the rest for you. If you prefer to do it yourself then read on. The embroidery will need to be backed by a piece of backing board (stiff card) which fits inside the frame (Fig 12). A white board is suitable for pale coloured fabrics but choose a toning card for dark colours. When framing behind a mount I sometimes just stick the embroidery to the card around the extreme edges. (Never allow glue on an area where it could be seen as a stain can develop over time.) I have used double-sided tape or occasionally staples.

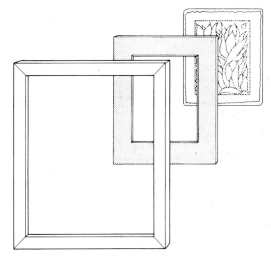

Fig 12 Framing embroidery with a mount.

If the piece is to be framed without a mount then it must be laced round the card. This method should also be used if you need to cure any wrinkles or distortions. Cut the backing card to fit easily inside the frame, remembering to allow for the thickness of fabric pulled round the edge. Mark the centre of each side on the back of the card. Mark where you want the centre of the embroidery to be by pins at the edges. Lay the front of the card on the wrong side of the fabric, matching the centre marks. Fold the fabric round the card and hold it in place by pushing pins through into the edge of the card (Fig 13). Start at the centres and work outwards on opposite sides. Every so often, turn the work over to check that the fabric is held taut and that the grain of the fabric is straight. When you are satisfied, take a long length of buttonhole or linen thread and lace from side to side, pulling the thread tightly enough to hold the fabric firmly in place without bending the card. Repeat this operation with the other two sides. This method is reversible, giving you the option of changing your mind later. I prefer to frame without glass, but if you choose to use it, ask the framer not to squash the glass up against the embroidery, flattening its texture.

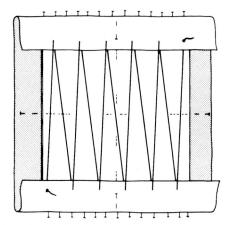

Fig 13 Lacing embroidery for framing without a mount.

Mitring a Corner

This is a neat way of removing excess fabric from a corner. Fold the fabric along the edges as far as required and mark the fold line. Unfold the turnings. At the corner, fold the fabric on the diagonal as shown in Fig 14. Press the crease. Allowing for a small turning along the creased side, trim away the excess fabric. Turn in the long edges and the creased diagonal sides should meet in a neat mitre. Stitch them together invisibly. See page 27 for details of mitring the corners of the Peacock Rug.

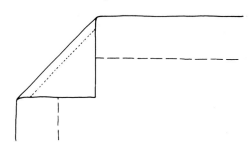

Fig 14 Mitring a corner.

Cushions

On the back of the embroidered fabric, mark exactly where you want the edge of the cushion to be, bearing in mind the sizes of cushion pad available. Choose a backing fabric that matches or tones with the embroidered fabric. Cut it to the finished size plus turnings, then place the fabrics right sides together and pin them. With the wrong side of the embroidered fabric uppermost, machine stitch following the marked edge line. Start a short distance from one corner, go round three sides and finish by stitching a little way round the last corner, leaving a gap to put the cushion pad through (Fig 15). Work another line of stitching round the corners to reinforce them, then cut diagonally across the corners, quite close to the stitching, and trim the other edges, leaving the usual seam allowance. Turn the cushion to the right side and press the seam. Insert the pad and invisibly stitch the edges together.

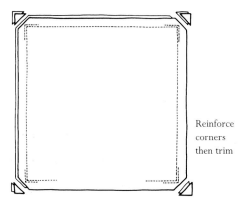

Reinforce corners then trim

Fig 15 Making a cushion cover.

An alternative method is to make up the backing piece with a zip inserted (Fig 16). To do this you need a slightly larger backing piece cut in half. Place the two halves right sides together. Sew 2in (5cm) of the seam at top and bottom and insert a zip in the gap. Proceed as above but sew round all four sides. Open the zip to turn the cushion and insert the pad. You could add cord or piping round the edges, for an attractive finish but this should be inserted before sewing the front to the back.

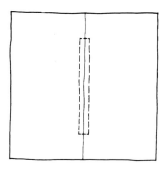

Fig 16 Backing fabric with zip inserted.

·BIBLIOGRAPHY·

Art Nouveau by Alastair Duncan (Thames and Hudson Ltd, 1994)

Art Nouveau by Lara-Vinca Masini (Thames and Hudson Ltd, 1994)

In the Nouveau Style by Malcolm Haslam (Thames and Hudson Ltd, 1989)

Art Nouveau, Spirit of the Belle Epoch by Susan A. Sternau (Tiger Books International, 1996)

Art Nouveau Graphic Art by Otto Lorenz (Berghaus, 1995)

Art Nouveau Floral Designs of Eugène Grasset, introduced by Laura Suffield (Bracken Books, 1988)

Full-colour Floral Designs in the Art Nouveau Style by E. A. Seguy, edited by C. R. Fry (Dover Publications, 1977)

The Victoria and Albert Museum's Textile Collection British Textiles from 1850–1900 by Linda Parry (Victoria and Albert Museum)

Arts and Crafts in Britain and America by Isabelle Anscombe and Charlotte Gere (Academy Editions, London, 1978)

Victorian Ceramic Tiles by Julian Barnard (Studio Vista, 1981)

The Aesthetic Movement by Lionel Lambourne (Phaidon Press Ltd, 1996)

The Designs of William de Morgan by Martin Greenwood (Richard Denis Publications, 1989)

Tiffany Windows by Alastair Duncan (Thames and Hudson, 1980)

Emile Gallé by Tim Newark (Apple Press, 1989)

The Art of René Lalique by P. Bayer and M. Waller (Grange Books, 1988)

Charles Rennie Mackintosh by Charlotte and Peter Fiell (Taschen, 1997)

Mackintosh Watercolours by Roger Billcliffe (John Murray, 1978)

Alphonse Mucha Edited by J. Hoole and T. Soto, introduced by Victor Arwas (Lund Humphries/Barbican Art Gallery, 1993)

Alphonse Maria Mucha by Jiri Mucha (Academy Editions, 1989)

Gustav Klimt by Gilles Neret (Taschen, 1993)

Archibald Knox Edited by Stephen Martin (Academy Editions, 1995)

Aubrey Beardsley by Stephen Calloway (V & A Publications, 1998)

·SUPPLIERS·

FABRICS
Zweigart fabrics from DMC stockists:
contact DMC Creative World Ltd, Pullman Road,
Wigston, Leicestershire LE18 2DY. Tel 0116 2811040
Fax 0116 2813592

Also by mail order from Willow Fabrics, 95 Town Lane,
Mobberley, Cheshire WA16 7HH.
Tel Freephone 0800 0567811
Web www.willowfabrics.com

In the USA from Joan Toggitt Ltd, 2 Riverview Drive,
Somerset, NJ 08873. Tel 908 2711949
Fax 908 2710758

In Australia from DMC 51–66 Carrington Road,
Marrickville, New South Wales 2204.
Tel 00612 559 3088

In New Zealand from Warnaar Trading Co Ltd, 376
Ferry Road, PO Box 19567, Christchurch.
Tel 0064 38 92 88

Fabric Flair fabrics from needlework shops.
Contact Fabric Flair Ltd, The Old Brewery,
The Close, Warminster, Wiltshire BA12 9AL.
Tel Freephone 0800 716 851 Fax 01985 846849

Permin Fabrics from needlework shops. Contact
Michael Whitaker Fabrics Ltd, 15/16 Midland Mills,
Station Road, Crosshills, near Keighley, West Yorkshire
BD20 7DT. Tel 01535 636903
Fax 01535 636431

Metallic gauze fabrics from various outlets
including dress fabric shops.
By Mail Order from Fantasy Fabrics, Duich Lodge,
Croyard Road, Beaulay, Scotland IV4 7DG
Tel/Fax 01463 783606

THREADS
DMC threads in the UK, Australia and New Zealand
from the stockists listed above.

In the USA from the DMC Corporation, 10 Port Kearny,
South Kearny, NJ 07032-4612.
Tel 201 589 0606

Anchor stranded cotton, wool and Kreinik metallic
threads from Coats Craft stockists. Contact Coats Craft
UK, PO Box 22, The Lingfield Estate, McMullen Rd,
Darlington, County Durham DL1 1YQ.
Tel 01325 365457 Fax 01325 394200

In the USA contact Coats and Clark, Greenville, SC. Tel
800 243 08 10 Fax 864 877 61 17

In Australia contact Coats Patons Craft, Mulgrave 3170.
Tel 03 9561 2288 Fax 03 9561 2298

In New Zealand contact Coats Spencer Crafts, East
Tamaki. Tel 09 274 01 16 Fax 09 274 05 84

Kreinik metallic threads in the USA contact Kreinik
Manufacturing Co Inc 3106 Titmanus Lane, Suite#101,
Baltimore, MD 21244. Tel 1 800 537 2166

Madeira threads from needlework shops or by mail
order from Barnyarns Ltd, PO Box 28, Thirsk, North
Yorkshire YO7 3YN. Tel 01845 524344
Fax 01845 525046

In the USA from Madeira (USA) Ltd, PO Box 6068, 30
Bayside Court, Laconia, NH03246. Tel 603 5282944 Fax
603 528 4264

ACCESSORIES
Trinket pots, coasters, pen holder, notebook cover,
wooden base pincushion and Mill Hill beads from
Framecraft Miniatures Ltd, 372–376 Summer Lane,
Hockley, Birmingham B19 3QA. Tel 0121 212 0551
Fax 0121 212 0552

In the USA from Anne Brinkley Designs, 761 Palmer
Avenue, Holmdel NJ 07733. Tel 908 787 2011
or Gay Bowles Sales Inc, PO Box 1060, Janesville, WIS
53547. Tel 608 754 9212 Fax 608 754 0665

In Australia contact Ireland Needlecraft Pty Ltd, 2–4
Keppel Drive, Hallam, Victoria 3808. Tel 03 702 3222

Clock kit for the Mackintosh rose clock from Glyn
Owen, Afallon, Church Hill, Glyn Ceiriog, Llangollen
LL20 7DN. Tel and Fax 01691 718579

Clock components for the Voysey landscape clock
from Glyn Owen as above or
C & L Clocks, King's Hill Industrial Estate, Bude,
Cornwall. Tel 01288 353351 Fax 01288 353135
or
Yorkshire Clock Builders, 654 Chesterfield Road,
Woodseats, Sheffield S8 0SB. Tel 0114 255 0786

Work-box by Market Square Warminster Ltd, Wing
Farm, Longbridge Deverill, Warminster, Wiltshire BA12
7DD. Tel 01985 841041 Fax 01985 541042

·ACKNOWLEDGEMENTS·

COMPLETING THIS BOOK would have been impossible without the invaluable help of so many people. I am particularly grateful to the embroiderers who have been so generous with their skill and time. I've set them very challenging deadlines and they have met them with speed, accuracy and enthusiasm. I want to thank Barbara Barnes for the anemone lady and the Tiffany work-box; Betty Coggins for the Mackintosh rose clock; Brenda Francis for the tulip picture; Carole Smith for the daffodil lady; Diana Hogg for the poppy lady; Edith Rackham for the rose lady picture; Geoffrey Howson for the bolster cushion bands; Hilary Heatherington for the columbine picture and the daffodil border; Joan Harris for the champagne lady, art is the flower picture, flying crane desk set and little lily picture; June Inman for a Mackintosh rose cushion and a number of borders; Kay King for the pillowslip and the rose card; Muriel Gray for the sunflower table mat, a Mackintosh rose cushion and several borders; Rosie Minors for the snowdrop cushion; Valerie Ray for the Klimt mirror frame and the Voysey landscape clock; Yvonne Tudgay for the lake landscape picture; and an enormous thank you to Stephanie and Christopher Bramwell who stitched the peacock rug between them and made a really lovely job of it in a record-breaking time. All the embroiderers have done beautiful work and I could not have managed without them.

Companies have been very helpful and generous in providing materials and accessories. My thanks to DMC for fabrics and threads and especially to Cara for her advice; to Coats for a variety of threads and wools; to Fabric Flair for fabrics; Framecraft for accessories including the pincushion, coasters, decorative pots, notebook cover and pen holder; and to Glyn Owen who have created a case for the Mackintosh clock. Technical help has been provided unstintingly by Colin Fulford of Easy Cross software.

My thanks to my editor, Cheryl Brown, for allowing me to indulge my interest in Art Nouveau and for all her help and encouragement and to Brenda Morrison and Lin Clements for all their hard work in getting the book into shape. I would also like to thank Diana Knapp for the book design and Tim Hill for his lovely evocative photographs.

Acknowledgements and thanks go to the following for the use of their images: page 8 La Dame aux Camélias (Copyright © Mucha Trust 1999); page 11 Tiffany Blossom, Goldfish Bowl and Parrots Window (Christies Images Ltd 1999); page 38 Portrait of Adele Bloch-Bauer (AKG London); page 96 Margaret Macdonald's appliquéd panel (Collection: Glasgow School of Art). Thanks also to: Christopher Wray for the Tiffany lamps used on pages 13, 53 and 91; and to Bracken Books for the Grasset folio designs used in the book.

And last but not least, my thanks to all my family for their help and support.

·INDEX·

Page numbers in **bold** refer to charts; page numbers in italics refer to illustrations